PRACTICE – ASSESS – DIAGNOSE

180 Days of
LANGUAGE
for First Grade

- ✓ capitalization
- ✓ punctuation
- ✓ parts of speech
- ✓ spelling

Author
Christine Dugan, M.A.Ed.

SHELL EDUCATION

Image Credits

All images Shutterstock

Standards

© Copyright 2010. National Governors Association Center for Best Practices and Council of Chief State School Officers. All rights reserved.

Shell Education
5301 Oceanus Drive
Huntington Beach, CA 92649-1030
http://www.shelleducation.com
ISBN 978-1-4258-1166-2
© 2015 Shell Education Publishing, Inc.

TABLE OF CONTENTS

INTRODUCTION AND RESEARCH

People who love the English language often lament the loss of grammar knowledge and the disappearance of systematic grammar instruction. We wince at emails with errors, such as when the noun *advice* is used instead of the verb *advise*. We may set aside a résumé with the incorrect placement of an apostrophe. And some of us pore (not pour) over entertaining punctuation guides such as *Eats, Shoots and Leaves* by Lynne Truss (2003). We chuckle over collections of bloopers such as *Anguished English: An Anthology of Accidental Assaults upon Our Language* by Richard Lederer (1987).

Even though we worry about grammar, our students arrive at school with a complex set of grammar rules in place—albeit affected by the prevailing dialect (Hillocks and Smith 2003, 727). For example, while students may not be able to recite the rule for where to position an adjective, they know intuitively to say *the yellow flower* instead of *the flower yellow.* All this knowledge comes without formal instruction. Further, young people easily shift between articulating or writing traditional patterns of grammar and communicating complete sentences with startling efficiency: IDK (I don't know), and for the ultimate in brevity, K (okay).

So, if students speak fairly well and have already mastered a complex written shorthand, why study grammar? Researchers provide us with three sound reasons:

1. the insights it offers into the way the language works

2. its usefulness in mastering standard forms of English

3. its usefulness in improving composition skills (Hillocks and Smith 1991, 594)

INTRODUCTION AND RESEARCH *(cont.)*

Studying grammar also provides users—teachers, students, and parents—with a common vocabulary to discuss both spoken and written language. The Assembly for the Teaching of English Grammar states, "Grammar is important because it is the language that makes it possible for us to talk about language. Grammar names the types of words and word groups that make up sentences not only in English but in any language. As human beings, we can put sentences together even as children—we all *do* grammar. But to be able to talk about how sentences are built, about the types of words and word groups that make up sentences—that is *knowing about* grammar."

With the publication of the Common Core State Standards, key instructional skills are identified, such as identifying parts of speech, using prepositional phrases, capitalizing, and correctly using commas. Writing conventions such as punctuation serve an important function for the reader— setting off syntactic units and providing intonational cues and semantic information. Capitalization provides the reader with such cues as sentence beginnings and proper nouns (Hodges 1991, 779).

The Need for Practice

To be successful in today's classroom, students must deeply understand both concepts and procedures so that they can discuss and demonstrate their understanding. Demonstrating understanding is a process that must be continually practiced in order for students to be successful. According to Marzano, "practice has always been, and always will be, a necessary ingredient to learning procedural knowledge at a level at which students execute it independently" (2010, 83). Practice is especially important to help students apply their concrete, conceptual understanding of a particular language skill.

Understanding Assessment

In addition to providing opportunities for frequent practice, teachers must be able to assess students' comprehension and word-study skills. This is important so that teachers can adequately address students' misconceptions, build on their current understanding, and challenge them appropriately. Assessment is a long-term process that often involves careful analysis of student responses from a lesson discussion, project, practice sheet, or test. When analyzing the data, it is important for teachers to reflect on how their teaching practices may have influenced students' responses, and to identify those areas where additional instruction may be required. In short, the data gathered from assessments should be used to inform instruction: slow down, speed up, or reteach. This type of assessment is called *formative assessment*.

HOW TO USE THIS BOOK

With *180 Days of Language,* students receive practice with punctuation, identifying parts of speech, capitalization, and spelling. The daily practice will develop students' writing efforts and oral reading skills.

Easy to Use and Standards-Based

These activities reinforce grade-level skills across a variety of language concepts. The questions are provided as a full practice page, making them easy to prepare and implement as part of a classroom morning routine, at the beginning of each language arts lesson, or as homework.

Every practice page provides questions that are tied to a language standard. Students are given opportunities for regular practice in language skills, allowing them to build confidence through these quick standards-based activities.

Question	Language Skill	Common Core State Standard
1	capitalization	**Language.1.2.a**—Capitalize dates and names of people.
2	punctuation	**Language.1.2.b**—Use end punctuation for sentences. **Language.1.2.c**—Use commas in dates and to separate single words in a series.
3	parts of speech	**Language.1.1.b**—Use common, proper, and possessive nouns. **Language.1.1.c**—Use singular and plural nouns with matching verbs in basic sentences. **Language.1.1.d**—Use personal, possessive, and indefinite pronouns. **Language.1.1.e**—Use verbs to convey a sense of past, present, and future. **Language.1.1.f**—Use frequently occurring adjectives. **Language.1.1.g**—Use frequently occurring conjunctions.
4	spelling	**Language.1.2.d**—Use conventional spelling for words with common spelling patterns for frequently occurring irregular words. **Language.1.2.c**—Spell untaught words phonetically, drawing on phonemic awareness and spelling conventions.

HOW TO USE THIS BOOK *(cont.)*

Using the Practice Pages

Practice pages provide instruction and assessment opportunities for each day of the school year. Teachers may wish to prepare packets of weekly practice pages for the classroom or for homework. As outlined on page 5, every question is aligned to a language skill.

Practice pages provide instruction and assessment opportunities for each day of the school year.

Each question ties student practice to a specific language skill.

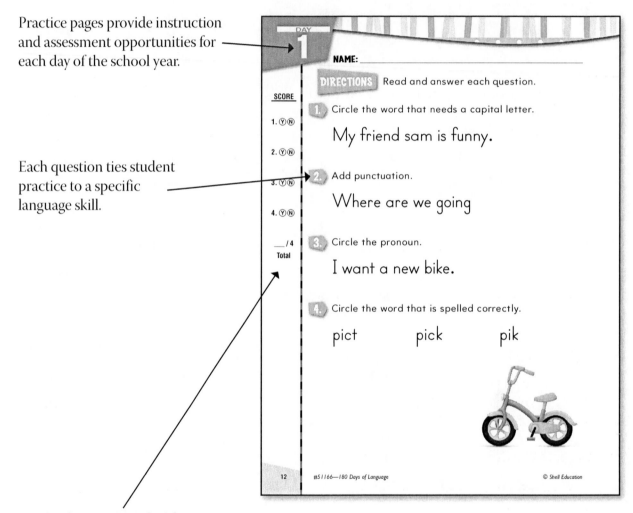

Using the Scoring Guide

Use the scoring guide along the side of each practice page to check answers and see at a glance which skills may need more reinforcement.

Fill in the appropriate circle for each problem to indicate correct (Y) or incorrect (N) responses. You might wish to indicate only incorrect responses to focus on those skills. (For example, if students consistently miss items 2 and 4, they may need additional help with those concepts as outlined in the table on page 5.) Use the answer key at the back of the book to score the problems, or you may call out answers to have students self-score or peer-score their work.

HOW TO USE THIS BOOK (cont.)

Diagnostic Assessment

Teachers can use the practice pages as diagnostic assessments. The data analysis tools included with the book enable teachers or parents to quickly score students' work and monitor their progress. Teachers and parents can see at a glance which language skills students may need to target in order to develop proficiency.

After students complete a practice page, grade each page using the answer key (pages 192–199). Then, complete the *Practice Page Item Analysis* for the appropriate day (page 8) for the whole class, or the *Student Item Analysis* (page 9) for individual students. These charts are also provided on the Digital Resource CD as PDFs, Microsoft Word® files, and as Microsoft Excel® files (filenames: pageitem.pdf, pageitem.doc, pageitem.xls; studentitem.pdf, studentitem.doc, studentitem.xls). Teachers can input data into the electronic files directly on the computer, or they can print the pages and analyze students' work using paper and pencil.

To complete the Practice Page Item Analyses:

- Write or type students' names in the far-left column. Depending on the number of students, more than one copy of the form may be needed, or you may need to add rows.

- The item numbers are included across the top of the chart. Each item correlates with the matching question number from the practice page.

- For each student, record an *X* in the column if the student has the item incorrect. If the item is correct, leave the space in the column blank.

- If you are using the Excel file, totals will be automatically generated. If you are using the Word file or if you have printed the PDF, you will need to compute the totals. Count the Xs in each row and column and fill in the correct boxes.

To complete the Student Item Analyses:

- Write or type the student's name on the top row. This form tracks the ongoing progress of each student, so one copy per student is necessary.

- The item numbers are included across the top of the chart. Each item correlates with the matching question number from the practice page.

- For each day, record an *X* in the column if the student has the item incorrect. If the item is correct, leave the space in the column blank.

- If you are using the Excel file, totals will be automatically generated. If you are using the Word file or if you have printed the PDF, you will need to compute the totals. Count the Xs in each row and column and fill in the correct boxes.

HOW TO USE THIS BOOK (cont.)

Practice Page Item Analysis

Directions: Record an *X* in cells to indicate where students have missed questions. Add up the totals. You can view: (1) which questions/concepts were missed per student; (2) the total correct score for each student; and (3) the total number of students who missed each question.

Day: _____ Question #	1	2	3	4	# correct
Student Name					
Sample Student	x				3/4
# of students missing each question					

HOW TO USE THIS BOOK (cont.)

Student Item Analysis

Directions: Record an *X* in cells to indicate where the student has missed questions. Add up the totals. You can view: (1) which questions/concepts the student missed; (2) the total correct score per day; and (3) the total number of times each question/concept was missed.

Student Name: Sample Student					
Question	1	2	3	4	# correct
Day					
1		X			3/4
Total					

HOW TO USE THIS BOOK (cont.)

Using the Results to Differentiate Instruction

Once results are gathered and analyzed, teachers can use the results to inform the way they differentiate instruction. The data can help determine which concepts are the most difficult for students and which need additional instructional support and continued practice. Depending on how often the practice pages are scored, results can be considered for instructional support on a daily or weekly basis.

Whole-Class Support

The results of the diagnostic analysis may show that the entire class is struggling with a particular concept or group of concepts. If these concepts have been taught in the past, this indicates that further instruction or reteaching is necessary. If these concepts have not been taught in the past, this data is a great preassessment and may demonstrate that students do not have a working knowledge of the concepts. Thus, careful planning for the length of the unit(s) or lesson(s) must be considered, and additional front-loading may be required.

Small-Group or Individual Support

The results of the diagnostic analysis may show that an individual or a small group of students is struggling with a particular concept or group of concepts. If these concepts have been taught in the past, this indicates that further instruction or reteaching is necessary. Consider pulling aside these students while others are working independently to instruct further on the concept(s). Teachers can also use the results to help identify individuals or groups of proficient students who are ready for enrichment or above-grade-level instruction. These students may benefit from independent learning contracts or more challenging activities. Students may also benefit from extra practice using games or computer-based resources.

My Language Book

Make copies of the *My Language Book* (pages 200–206) for students. Depending on students' abilities, have them reference this book while working on the activity pages.

Digital Resource CD

The Digital Resource CD provides all of the activity pages and all of the diagnostic pages in this book. The list of resources on the CDcan be found on page 208.

STANDARDS CORRELATIONS

Shell Education is committed to producing educational materials that are research and standards based. In this effort, we have correlated all of our products to the academic standards of all 50 states, the District of Columbia, the Department of Defense Dependents Schools, and all Canadian provinces.

How to Find Standards Correlations

To print a customized correlation report of this product for your state, visit our website at http://www.shelleducation.com and follow the on-screen directions. If you require assistance in printing correlation reports, please contact our Customer Service Department at 1-877-777-3450.

Purpose and Intent of Standards

Legislation mandates that all states adopt academic standards that identify the skills students will learn in kindergarten through grade twelve. Many states also have standards for Pre–K. This same legislation sets requirements to ensure the standards are detailed and comprehensive.

Standards are designed to focus instruction and guide adoption of curricula. Standards are statements that describe the criteria necessary for students to meet specific academic goals. They define the knowledge, skills, and content students should acquire at each level. Standards are also used to develop standardized tests to evaluate students' academic progress. Teachers are required to demonstrate how their lessons meet state standards. State standards are used in the development of all of our products, so educators can be assured they meet the academic requirements of each state.

Common Core State Standards

The activities in this book are aligned to the Common Core State Standards (CCSS). The chart on page 5 lists the standards. The chart is also on the Digital Resource CD (filename: standards.pdf).

NAME: _____

DIRECTIONS Read and answer each question.

1. Circle the word that needs a capital letter.

1. Ⓨ Ⓝ

My friend sam is funny.

2. Ⓨ Ⓝ

2. Add punctuation.

Where are we going

3. Ⓨ Ⓝ

3. Circle the pronoun.

4. Ⓨ Ⓝ

I want a new bike.

___ / 4
Total

4. Circle the word that is spelled correctly.

pict   pick   pik

NAME: _____

DIRECTIONS Read and answer each question.

1. Circle the word that needs a capital letter.

School will start on august 25.

2. Add punctuation.

I like to play soccer at recess

3. Write the correct noun.

The _____ feel sad today.
(**girls** or **girl**)

4. Circle the word that is spelled correctly.

yuse   yous   use

NAME: _____

DIRECTIONS Read and answer each question.

SCORE

1. Ⓨ Ⓝ

2. Ⓨ Ⓝ

3. Ⓨ Ⓝ

4. Ⓨ Ⓝ

___ / 4
Total

1. Write today's date using a capital letter.

_____

– – – – – – – – – – – – – – – – –

_____

2. Add punctuation.

The music is loud

3. Write the correct verb.

_____
Each day, I – – – – – – – – – – to school.
(**walking** or **walk**)

4. Circle the word that is spelled correctly.

gurin   grin   gren

 #51166—180 Days of Language

NAME: _____

DIRECTIONS Read and answer each question.

1. Circle the word that needs a capital letter.

Mrs. walker is my teacher.

1. Ⓨ Ⓝ

2. Add punctuation.

Where is my book

2. Ⓨ Ⓝ

3. Circle the adjective.

I like to sit in red chairs.

3. Ⓨ Ⓝ

4. Ⓨ Ⓝ

___ / 4
Total

4. Circle the word that is spelled correctly.

feeding   feedeing   feding

NAME: _____

DIRECTIONS   Read and answer each question.

1. Circle the word that needs a capital letter.

My friend lily was not at school.

2. Add punctuation.

I ate a lot at lunch

3. Write the correct verb.

Yesterday, I _____ pizza.
(eat or **ate)**

4. Circle the word that is spelled correctly.

you   yu   yoo

NAME: _____

DIRECTIONS Read and answer each question.

1. Circle the words that need capital letters.

Today, I will see dr. martin.

2. Add punctuation.

The cat is on the bed

3. Write the correct pronoun.

Dad told _____ to go to sleep.
(**me** or **I**)

4. Circle the word that is spelled correctly.

step   stepp   stap

NAME: _____

1. Ⓨ Ⓝ

2. Ⓨ Ⓝ

3. Ⓨ Ⓝ

4. Ⓨ Ⓝ

___ / 4
Total

DIRECTIONS Read and answer each question.

1. Circle the word that needs a capital letter.

The ball game is on may 25.

2. Add punctuation.

When is recess

3. Write the correct pronoun.

_____

_ _ _ _ _ _ _ _ reads the book.

(**He** or **They**)

4. Circle the word that is spelled correctly.

bist   best   beste

NAME: _____

DIRECTIONS Read and answer each question.

1. Circle the word that needs a capital letter.

I sit next to tim.

2. Add punctuation.

I am very excited today

3. Write the possessive noun.

_____

_ _ _ _ _ _ _ _ _ _ _ dog was missing.
_____
(belonging to Zoe)

4. Circle the word that is spelled correctly.

hawp   hopp   hop

NAME: _____

DIRECTIONS Read and answer each question.

1. Ⓨ Ⓝ

1. Circle the word that needs a capital letter.

The party is on july 6.

2. Ⓨ Ⓝ

2. Add commas.

I love bananas apples and melons.

3. Ⓨ Ⓝ

3. Write the adjective.

The _____ park was a lot of fun.
(**big** or **ran**)

4. Ⓨ Ⓝ

___/ 4
Total

4. Circle the word that is spelled correctly.

jet   jett   juet

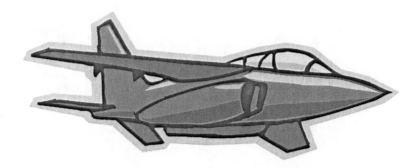

NAME: _____

DIRECTIONS Read and answer each question.

1. Circle the word that needs a capital letter.

My sister greta is nice.

2. Add commas.

I got books pencils and markers at the store.

3. Write the correct verb.

Yesterday, I _____

(**spell** or **spelled**)

all of the words.

4. Circle the word that is spelled correctly.

fiks   ficks   fix

NAME: _____

SCORE

1. Ⓨ Ⓝ

2. Ⓨ Ⓝ

3. Ⓨ Ⓝ

4. Ⓨ Ⓝ

___ / 4
Total

DIRECTIONS Read and answer each question.

1. Complete the sentence with a name.

_____

My friend _ _ _ _ _ _ _ _ _ _ _ _ is nice.

2. Add a comma.

School starts on August 24 2016.

3. Circle the nouns.

Put the food on the table.

4. Circle the word that is spelled correctly.

dep   deap   deep

NAME: _____

Read and answer each question.

1. Rewrite the sentence using correct capitalization.

dr. kim checks my teeth.

_____
- - - - - - - - - - - - -
_____
- - - - - - - - - - - - -
_____

2. Write the date of your birthday. Include a comma.

_____
- - - - - - - - - - - - -
_____

3. Circle the adjective.

Silly songs make me laugh.

4. Circle the word that is spelled correctly.

bone   boan   boyne

NAME: _____

DIRECTIONS Read and answer each question.

1. Ⓨ Ⓝ

1. Rewrite the sentence using correct capitalization.

Is my party in march or april?

_____

_ _ _ _ _ _ _ _ _ _ _ _ _ _ _ _ _

_____

_ _ _ _ _ _ _ _ _ _ _ _ _ _ _ _ _

_____

2. Ⓨ Ⓝ

3. Ⓨ Ⓝ

4. Ⓨ Ⓝ

___/ 4
Total

2. Add a comma.

Our trip is on June 5   201 6.

3. Write the possessive noun.

_____
Will you wash _ _ _ _ _ _ _ _ car?
              (belonging to Dad)

4. Circle the word that is spelled correctly.

tyme   tiam   time

NAME: _____

DIRECTIONS Read and answer each question.

1. Complete the sentence.

My teacher's name is

_____

‒ ‒ ‒ ‒ ‒ ‒ ‒ ‒ ‒ ‒ ‒ ‒

_____ .

2. Add punctuation.

The bus stopped

3. Write the correct pronoun.

_____

‒ ‒ ‒ ‒ ‒ ‒

_____ runs to the door.

(**He** or **They**)

4. Circle the word that is **not** spelled correctly.

We need roap to tie the box.

NAME: _____

DIRECTIONS Read and answer each question.

1. Finish the sentence.

My friend's name is
_____
- - - - - - - - - - - - - - - - -
_____ .

2. Add punctuation.

Where is Liam

3. Write the preposition.

The desk is _____

(**between** or **before**)

Katy and me.

4. Circle the word that is **not** spelled correctly.

Can I go wyth Jessie?

NAME: _____

DIRECTIONS Read and answer each question.

1. Add a name to complete the sentence.

My friend _____ is funny.

2. Add a comma.

The puppy was born on October 4 2016.

3. Write the possessive noun.

The _____ tail is long.
   (**horses** or **horse's**)

4. Circle the word that is spelled correctly.

fet   feet   feit

NAME: _____

DIRECTIONS Read and answer each question.

1. Ⓨ Ⓝ

2. Ⓨ Ⓝ

3. Ⓨ Ⓝ

4. Ⓨ Ⓝ

___/ 4
Total

1. Write the word with a capital letter.

_____
___ ___ ___ am good at math.
(i)

2. Add commas.

The car has doors wheels

and an engine.

3. Circle the adjective.

Pillows are fluffy.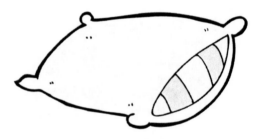

4. Circle the word that is spelled correctly.

sok   soc   sock

NAME: _____

DIRECTIONS Read and answer each question.

1. Circle the word that needs a capital letter.

I play with john at recess.

2. Add commas.

We use paint paper and glue at art time.

3. Circle the nouns.

I saw Mr. Cortez in the classroom.

4. Circle the word that is spelled correctly.

doing   dooing   dowing

NAME: _____

SCORE

1. Ⓨ Ⓝ

2. Ⓨ Ⓝ

3. Ⓨ Ⓝ

4. Ⓨ Ⓝ

___ / 4
Total

1. Rewrite the sentence using correct capitalization.

Our librarian is mr. perez.

_____

_ _ _ _ _ _ _ _ _ _ _ _ _ _ _

_____

_ _ _ _ _ _ _ _ _ _ _ _ _ _ _

_____

2. Write tomorrow's date. Include a comma.

_____

_ _ _ _ _ _ _ _ _ _ _ _ _ _ _

_____

3. Write the correct verb.

Yesterday, I $\underline{}$ a lot of fruit.
(**eat** or **ate**)

4. Circle the word that is spelled correctly.

scip   sckip   skip

NAME: _____

DIRECTIONS Read and answer each question.

1. Rewrite the sentence using correct capitalization.

we are going on a trip.

_____

- - - - - - - - - - - - - - - - -

_____

- - - - - - - - - - - - - - - - -

_____

2. Add punctuation.

Come home right now

3. Write the correct verb.

Yesterday, Anna _____

(laughs or laughed)

at her friend.

4. Circle the word that is spelled correctly.

slaam   slam   slamm

NAME: _____

DIRECTIONS Read and answer each question.

1. Circle the words that need capital letters.

1. Ⓨ Ⓝ

Is june or july your favorite month?

2. Ⓨ Ⓝ

2. Add punctuation.

3. Ⓨ Ⓝ

When is school over

4. Ⓨ Ⓝ

___ / 4
Total

3. Write the noun.

The _____ ran away.
    (cat or **skip)**

4. Circle the word that is spelled correctly.

see   sei   sey

 #51166—180 Days of Language

NAME: _____

DIRECTIONS Read and answer each question.

1. Circle the words that need capital letters.

She played with rose and ted.

2. Add commas.

The cake was made with eggs milk and butter.

3. Write the verb.

The frog _____.
(**green** or **hops**)

4. Circle the word that is spelled correctly.

caim   came   caym

NAME: _____

DIRECTIONS Read and answer each question.

1. Circle the word that needs a capital letter.

My birthday month is february.

2. Add punctuation.

The dog ate his food

3. Write the correct verb.

Tomorrow, I will _____

(**keeps** or **keep**)

my promise.

4. Circle the word that is spelled correctly.

hop   hopp   haup

NAME: _____

DIRECTIONS Read and answer each question.

1. Circle the words that need capital letters.

I see that tim and rex

play together.

2. Add a comma.

We moved on March 4 2014.

3. Write the adjective.

The _____ book was very good.

(**new** or **girl**)

4. Circle the word that is spelled correctly.

gaiv   gayv   gave

NAME: _____

DIRECTIONS Read and answer each question.

1. Circle the word that needs a capital letter.

Today is the first day of october.

2. Add punctuation.

The circus was a lot of fun

3. Write the correct pronoun.

Chloe likes to play with _____.

(**me** or **she**)

4. Circle the word that is spelled correctly.

rode   rowd   roud

NAME: _____

DIRECTIONS Read and answer each question.

1. Circle the words that need capital letters.

My friends are evan and ned.

1. Ⓨ Ⓝ

2. Add punctuation.

Who is the line leader

2. Ⓨ Ⓝ

3. Ⓨ Ⓝ

3. Combine the two sentences. Include a comma and the word *but*.

School was over. The bus was

not there.

4. Ⓨ Ⓝ

___/ 4
Total

_____

‑ ‑ ‑ ‑ ‑ ‑ ‑ ‑ ‑ ‑ ‑ ‑ ‑ ‑ ‑ ‑ ‑ ‑

_____

‑ ‑ ‑ ‑ ‑ ‑ ‑ ‑ ‑ ‑ ‑ ‑ ‑ ‑ ‑ ‑ ‑ ‑

_____

4. Add an *-ing* ending to the base word *do*.

_____

‑ ‑ ‑ ‑ ‑ ‑ ‑ ‑ ‑ ‑ ‑ ‑ ‑ ‑ ‑ ‑ ‑ ‑

_____

NAME: _____

Read and answer each question.

SCORE

1. Ⓨ Ⓝ

2. Ⓨ Ⓝ

3. Ⓨ Ⓝ

4. Ⓨ Ⓝ

___ / 4
Total

1. Circle the word that needs a capital letter.

How many days are left
in march?

2. Add punctuation.

The music was very quiet

3. Circle the adjective.

Hot chocolate tastes good.

4. Add an -s ending to the base word *bug*.

_____

_ _ _ _ _ _ _

NAME: _____

DIRECTIONS Read and answer each question.

1. Circle the words that need capital letters.

I want to read with chris or eva.

2. Add a comma.

My sister was born on August 7 2014.

3. Write the future tense verb.

The sky _____ very cloudy.
(**will be** or **was**)

4. Add an -s ending to the base word *get*.

_____

_____

NAME: _____

Read and answer each question.

SCORE

1. Ⓨ Ⓝ

2. Ⓨ Ⓝ

3. Ⓨ Ⓝ

4. Ⓨ Ⓝ

___ / 4
Total

1. Circle the words that need capital letters.

will it be hot in may?

2. Add a comma.

Camp starts on July 12 2016.

3. Combine the sentences. Include a comma and the word *and*.

Snow was falling. The street

was quiet.

_____

_____

_____

4. Circle the word that is spelled correctly.

this   thiss   thise

NAME: _____

DIRECTIONS Read and answer each question.

1. Circle the words that need capital letters.

You must work with gus and frank.

2. Add commas.

I saw bugs grass and rocks at the park.

3. Write the correct pronoun.

Dad and I rode _____ bikes.

(**our** or **her**)

4. Add an *-ing* ending to the base word *tell*.

_____

_ _ _ _ _ _ _ _

_____

NAME: _____

1. Ⓨ Ⓝ

2. Ⓨ Ⓝ

3. Ⓨ Ⓝ

4. Ⓨ Ⓝ

___ / 4
Total

DIRECTIONS Read and answer each question.

1. Circle the words that need capital letters.

My neighbor is bob gomez.

2. Add punctuation.

The flower grew in the pot

3. Circle the adjective.

I see green grass outside.

4. Circle the word that is spelled correctly.

ride   ryde   ried

NAME: _____

DIRECTIONS   Read and answer each question.

1. Circle the word that needs a capital letter.

It is very cold in january.

2. Add a comma.

The carnival was on April 15 2013.

3. Combine the two sentences. Include a comma and the word *but*.

I have soccer practice. I am hungry.

_____

- -

_____

- -

_____

4. Add an *-ing* ending to the base word *read*.

_____

- -

_____

NAME: _____

SCORE

1. Ⓨ Ⓝ

2. Ⓨ Ⓝ

3. Ⓨ Ⓝ

4. Ⓨ Ⓝ

___ / 4
Total

1. Circle the words that should start with capital letters.

The bus driver today is alice walters.

2. Add commas.

I want ice cream a cherry and whipped cream.

3. Write the correct verb.

Yesterday, I _____ at home.
(**play** or **played**)

4. Circle the word that is spelled correctly.

frog   frogg   frawg

NAME: _____

DIRECTIONS Read and answer each question.

1. Rewrite the sentence using correct capitalization.

mrs. Holly evans works in

the cafeteria.

_____

- - - - - - - - - - - -

_____

- - - - - - - - - - - -

_____

2. Add punctuation.

When is my soccer game

3. Circle the adjective.

Large whales swim around.

4. Add an *-ed* ending to the base word *walk*.

_____

- - - - - - - - -

_____

NAME: _____

DIRECTIONS Read and answer each question.

1. Circle the words that need capital letters.

I am shy around dr. perry,

my dentist.

2. Add a comma.

What day of the week is

June 4 2014?

3. Write the correct noun.

The _____ dances to the song.
(**girl** or **girls**)

4. Add an *-ing* ending to the base word *keep*.

_____

- - - - - - - - - - - - - - - - - - -

_____

NAME: _____

DIRECTIONS Read and answer each question.

1. Write the sentence with correct capitalization.

june starts today.

_____

- - - - - - - - - - - - - - - -

_____

- - - - - - - - - - - - - - - -

_____

2. Add punctuation.

That music sure is loud

3. Circle the adjective.

I hear loud cars.

4. Circle the word that is spelled correctly.

spin   spinn   sppin

NAME: _____

Read and answer each question.

SCORE

1. Ⓨ Ⓝ

2. Ⓨ Ⓝ

3. Ⓨ Ⓝ

4. Ⓨ Ⓝ

___ / 4
Total

1. Circle the words that need capital letters.

chloe and troy work well together.

2. Add commas.

The jacket had pockets buttons and zippers.

3. Write the correct verb.

Yesterday, I _____

(**added** or **adds**)

numbers at math time.

4. Circle the word that is spelled correctly.

uv   uf   of

NAME: _____

DIRECTIONS Read and answer each question.

1. Which word needs a capital letter? Write it correctly on the line.

Next week is december 8.

_____

- - - - - - - - - - - - - - - - - - -

_____

1. Ⓨ Ⓝ

2. Ⓨ Ⓝ

3. Ⓨ Ⓝ

4. Ⓨ Ⓝ

2. Add punctuation.

The coat kept her warm

___/4
Total

3. Write the correct verb.

The spider _____ slowly.

(**moves** or **move**)

4. Add an -*ing* ending to the base word *see*.

_____

- - - - - - - - - - - - - - - -

_____

NAME: _____

SCORE

1. Ⓨ Ⓝ

2. Ⓨ Ⓝ

3. Ⓨ Ⓝ

4. Ⓨ Ⓝ

___ / 4
Total

1. Circle the word that needs a capital letter.

The month of january is first.

2. Add a comma.

Next Sunday is
September 12 2015.

3. Write the adjective.

The _____ butterfly flew.

(**pretty** or **wing**)

4. Circle the word that is spelled correctly.

noos   nos   nose

NAME: _____

| DIRECTIONS | Read and answer each question. |

1. Circle the words that need capital letters.

I will invite parker and timmy.

2. Add punctuation.

Where is Mom

3. Write the correct noun.

The _____ stops at the corner.
(**car** or **cars**)

4. Add an *-ing* ending to the base word *say*.

_____

_ _ _ _ _ _ _ _ _

_____

NAME: _____

#51166—180 Days of Language

SCORE

1. Ⓨ Ⓝ

2. Ⓨ Ⓝ

3. Ⓨ Ⓝ

4. Ⓨ Ⓝ

___ / 4
Total

DIRECTIONS Read and answer each question.

1. Circle the words that need capital letters.

My friends are iris and nina.

2. Add punctuation.

How do you do that

3. Write the noun.

The _____ zoomed by.
   (**small** or **bee**)

4. Write the correctly spelled word.

_____ is my lunch.
   (**This** or **Thys**)

NAME: _____

DIRECTIONS   Read and answer each question.

1. Circle the words that need capital letters.

When can I play with uncle frank?

2. Add commas.

The rug was blue red and green.

3. Write the correct noun.

The _____ look for food.
(snake or **snakes)**

4. Circle the word that is spelled correctly.

bus   lus   mus

NAME: _____

DIRECTIONS Read and answer each question.

1. Which word needs a capital letter? Write it correctly on the line.

Homework is due may 2.

_____

_____

2. Add punctuation.

Who needs to rest

3. Write the correct verb.

Yesterday, Mom _____
(**watched** or **watches**)

the baby.

4. Which word is spelled correctly?

_____ book makes me laugh.
(**That** or **Tat**)

NAME: _____

DIRECTIONS Read and answer each question.

1. Circle the word that needs a capital letter.

My friend justin is nice.

2. Add a comma.

How many days until January 3 2016?

3. Write the correct verb.

Each day, I _____
(**walked** or **walk**)

to the library.

4. Write the word that is spelled correctly.

I ride a _____ .
(**bike** or **byke**)

SCORE

1. Ⓨ Ⓝ

2. Ⓨ Ⓝ

3. Ⓨ Ⓝ

4. Ⓨ Ⓝ

___ / 4
Total

NAME: _____

DIRECTIONS Read and answer each question.

SCORE

1. Ⓨ Ⓝ

2. Ⓨ Ⓝ

3. Ⓨ Ⓝ

4. Ⓨ Ⓝ

___ / 4
Total

1. Circle the words that need capital letters.

My aunt ruth is funny.

2. Add commas to the sentence.

The story needs a beginning a middle and an end.

3. Write the adjective.

The _____ flower smells nice.
(small or **stem)**

4. Circle the word that is spelled correctly.

the   teh   thu

 #51166—180 Days of Language

NAME: _____

DIRECTIONS Read and answer each question.

1. Which word needs a capital letter? Write it on the line.

Tomorrow is march 3.

_____

_ _ _ _ _ _ _ _ _ _ _ _ _ _

_____

2. Add punctuation.

Where do I go

3. Choose the correct pronoun.

_____

_ _ _ _ _ _ _ _ _ _ _

Anna wanted

(**her** or **their**)

roller skates.

4. Circle the word that is spelled correctly.

sed   said   saed

NAME: _____

SCORE

1. Ⓨ Ⓝ

2. Ⓨ Ⓝ

3. Ⓨ Ⓝ

4. Ⓨ Ⓝ

___/ 4
Total

1. Circle the words that need capital letters.

Uncle joe and aunt pam are here.

2. Add punctuation.

That is very loud

3. Circle the adjective.

Trophies are shiny.

4. Circle the word that is spelled correctly.

an   ane   aan

#51166—180 Days of Language

NAME: _____

DIRECTIONS Read and answer each question.

1. Circle the word that needs a capital letter.

Can we go away on june 15?

2. Add commas.

The pie was made with milk sugar and flour.

3. Write the correct verb.

Yesterday, Ian _____

(**skip** or **skipped**)

his homework.

4. Circle the word that is spelled correctly.

com   cume   come

NAME: _____

DIRECTIONS Read and answer each question.

1. Circle the words that need capital letters.

Our table group includes max and brad.

2. Add punctuation.

I am very mad

3. Write the adjective.

The _____ fire was hot.

(**large** or **flame**)

4. Write the word that is spelled correctly.

I see a _____ go by.

(**bug** or **bugg**)

NAME: _____

DIRECTIONS   Read and answer each question.

1. Which word needs a capital letter? Write it correctly on the line.

Movie night is on may 29.

_ _

_____

2. Add commas.

Do you want chocolate vanilla or

strawberry ice cream?

3. Write the correct verb.

The rain _____ no recess.
(**mean** or **means**)

4. Write the word that is spelled correctly.

Can we _____ home?
(**runn** or **run**)

NAME: _____

DIRECTIONS Read and answer each question.

1. Circle the word that needs a capital letter.

i like pizza.

2. Add punctuation.

Do you like bugs

3. Circle the adjective.

Pretty flowers grow in parks.

4. Write the word that is spelled correctly.

Say _____ or no.
(**yes** or **yis**)

NAME: _____

Read and answer each question.

1. Circle the word that needs a capital letter.

Are you coming over, anna?

2. Add a comma.

My birthday is June 4 2016.

3. Write the past tense verb.

Today, I _____ a parrot.
(**see** or **saw**)

4. Write the word that is spelled correctly.

The _____ was fast.
(**gett** or **jet**)

1. Ⓨ Ⓝ

2. Ⓨ Ⓝ

3. Ⓨ Ⓝ

4. Ⓨ Ⓝ

___ / 4
Total

NAME: _____

Read and answer each question.

SCORE

1. Ⓨ Ⓝ

2. Ⓨ Ⓝ

3. Ⓨ Ⓝ

4. Ⓨ Ⓝ

___/4
Total

1. Which word needs a capital letter? Write it correctly on the line.

i am so hungry!

_____

_ _ _ _ _ _ _ _ _ _

_____

2. Add commas.

Riley Oscar and Jose are in line.

3. Write the correct verb.

Tomorrow, I _____ to her.
(**talk** or **will talk**)

4. Add an -ing ending to the base word *say*.

_____

_ _ _ _ _ _ _ _ _ _ _ _

_____

NAME: _____

DIRECTIONS Read and answer each question.

1. Circle the words that need capital letters.

I saw dr. evan and dr. parker at the store.

2. Add commas.

Hank Anna and Cole are on the bus.

3. Write the correct verb.

The ant _____ over the rock.
(step or **steps)**

4. Write the word that is spelled correctly.

The _____ of the pot was off.
(top or **topp)**

NAME: _____

SCORE

DIRECTIONS Read and answer each question.

1. (Y)(N)

1. Circle the words that need capital letters.

The play is on march 5 and march 6.

2. (Y)(N)

2. Add a comma.

Mark the calendar for January 5 2018.

3. (Y)(N)

4. (Y)(N)

4. Circle the adjective.

Classrooms are fun.

___/4
Total

4. Circle the word that is spelled correctly.

since   sence   sinse

NAME: _____

DIRECTIONS Read and answer each question.

1. Rewrite the sentence using correct capitalization.

the plane leaves on may 25.

_____

- - - - - - - - - - - - - - - - - -

_____

- - - - - - - - - - - - - - - - - -

_____

2. Add punctuation.

The rose is red

3. Circle the adjective.

Nina loves stuffed bears.

4. Add an *-ing* ending to the base word *camp*.

_____

- - - - - - - - - - - - - - - - - -

_____

NAME: _____

DIRECTIONS Read and answer each question.

SCORE

1. Ⓨ Ⓝ

2. Ⓨ Ⓝ

3. Ⓨ Ⓝ

4. Ⓨ Ⓝ

___ / 4
Total

1. Circle the words that need capital letters.

Will I see mr. roberts today?

2. Add punctuation.

I need a new hat

3. Write the correct verb.

Amanda _____ a dollar bill.
(**find** or **finds**)

4. Write the word that is spelled correctly.

I see the _____ in the coat.
(**rip** or **ryp**)

NAME: _____

DIRECTIONS Read and answer each question.

1. Circle the words that need capital letters.

I love my grandpa joe and my grandma alana.

2. Add punctuation.

When is school out

3. Write the correct pronoun.

Can you help out while

_____ go away?

(**she** or **we**)

4. Write the word that is spelled correctly.

Can the dog _____ over?

(**flip** or **flap**)

NAME: _____

DIRECTIONS Read and answer each question.

1. Rewrite the sentence using correct capitalization.

can we have a party on may 15?

- -

_____

_____

- -

_____

2. Add punctuation.

How are you doing

3. Write the adjective.

The _____ sunrise was pretty.
   (**early** or **sun**)

4. Write the correct word.

I like the _____ of the story.
   (**and** or **end**)

NAME: _____

DIRECTIONS Read and answer each question.

1. Circle the words that need capital letters.

paul, ron, and taylor are coming over.

2. Add punctuation.

I am very happy

3. Write the present tense verb.

The girl _____ home.
(walks or **walked)**

4. Circle the word that is spelled correctly.

jobb   job   jowb

NAME: _____

DIRECTIONS Read and answer each question.

1. What is today's date? Use a capital letter.

_____

- - - - - - - - - - - - -

_____

2. Add punctuation.

I cannot wait for summer

3. Combine the two sentences. Include a comma and the word *but*.

The baby will sleep. First he needs milk.

_____

- - - - - - - - - - - - -

_____

- - - - - - - - - - - - -

_____

4. Write the correct word.

My _____ keeps running.

(noze or **nose)**

NAME: _____

DIRECTIONS Read and answer each question.

1. Circle the word that needs a capital letter.

let's go for a walk.

2. Add punctuation.

Where is my hat

3. Circle the nouns.

The girl walked to her house.

4. Add an *-ing* ending to the base word *go*.

_____

_ _ _ _ _ _ _ _

_____

NAME: _____

DIRECTIONS Read and answer each question.

SCORE

1. Ⓨ Ⓝ

2. Ⓨ Ⓝ

3. Ⓨ Ⓝ

4. Ⓨ Ⓝ

___ / 4
Total

1. Circle the word that needs a capital letter.

Is paul out sick today?

2. Add punctuation.

That really hurt

3. Write the plural noun.

The _____ are happy.
(**dog** or **dogs**)

4. Write the correct word.

Please _____ the yard.
(**raik** or **rake**)

NAME: _____

DIRECTIONS   Read and answer each question.

1. Circle the word that needs a capital letter.

Our coach, mario, was

happy today.

2. Add punctuation.

The lizard is green

3. Write the correct noun.

The _____ sits at the desk.
(**child** or **child's**)
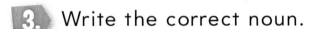

4. Circle the word that is spelled correctly.

know   nowe   knouw

NAME: _____

1. Ⓨ Ⓝ

2. Ⓨ Ⓝ

3. Ⓨ Ⓝ

4. Ⓨ Ⓝ

___ / 4
Total

DIRECTIONS Read and answer each question.

1. Circle the words that need capital letters.

Did nurse chris come in yet?

2. Add punctuation.

The water is cold

3. Combine the two sentences. Add the word *because.*

I like to wake up early. I like mornings.

_____

_____

_____

_____

_____

_____

4. Circle the word that is spelled correctly.

kan   can   cann

NAME: _____

| DIRECTIONS | Read and answer each question. |

1. Add a name to the sentence.

_____

I will play with _____.

2. Add commas.

We had food towels and toys

at the beach.

3. Write the correct verb.

_____

The class _____ a game.
              (**play** or **plays**)

4. Circle the word that is spelled correctly.

opn   open   opin

NAME: _____

DIRECTIONS   Read and answer each question.

1.   Circle the words that need capital letters.

My piano teacher is mrs. oliver.

2.   Add a comma.

February 14 2016

3.   Circle the adjective.

Friends are nice.

4.   Circle the word that is spelled correctly.

soc   sock   sok

NAME: _____

DIRECTIONS Read and answer each question.

1. Add a name to the sentence.

I work well with _____.

2. Add commas.

Green red and blue are my favorite colors.

3. Circle the pronoun.

I went inside with Mary.

4. Add an *-ing* ending to the base word *help*.

_____

NAME: _____

DIRECTIONS Read and answer each question.

1. Circle the word that needs a capital letter.

november 29, 2016

2. Add commas.

June 18 2015 will be a great day.

3. Write the correct verb.

The team _____ the game.
(**lose** or **lost**)

4. Circle the word that is spelled correctly.

agen   again   ugen

#51166—180 Days of Language   © Shell Education

NAME: _____

DIRECTIONS Read and answer each question.

1. Add a name to the sentence.

I think _____ works hard.

2. Add commas.

Let's make a fort out of pillows blankets and towels.

3. Circle the verb.

I went under the desk.

4. Circle the word that is spelled correctly.

thank   thanck   thaink

SCORE

1. Ⓨ Ⓝ
2. Ⓨ Ⓝ
3. Ⓨ Ⓝ
4. Ⓨ Ⓝ

___ / 4
Total

NAME: _____

DIRECTIONS Read and answer each question.

1. Circle the word that needs a capital letter.

Today is january 4, 2015.

2. Add a comma.

December 25 2015

3. Write the past tense verb.

The bird _____ its wings.

(**moves** or **moved**)

4. Circle the word that is spelled correctly.

give   giv   gyv

NAME: _____

DIRECTIONS Read and answer each question.

1. What is tomorrow's date? Use a capital letter.

_____

– – – – – – – – – – – – – – – –

_____

1. Ⓨ Ⓝ

2. Ⓨ Ⓝ

2. Add commas.

Mom put cheese an apple
and chips in my lunch.

3. Ⓨ Ⓝ

4. Ⓨ Ⓝ

___/ 4
Total

3. Write the correct verb.

I will _____ in the car.
(**stay** or **stays**)

4. Circle the word that is spelled correctly.

whenn   wen   when

NAME: _____

SCORE

1. Ⓨ Ⓝ

2. Ⓨ Ⓝ

3. Ⓨ Ⓝ

4. Ⓨ Ⓝ

___/4
Total

1. Which word needs a capital letter? Write it correctly on the line.

Today is tuesday.

_____

- - - - - - - - - - - - - - - -

_____

2. Add a comma.

August 1 2000

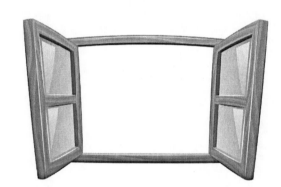

3. Circle the nouns.

The bird flew out of the window.

4. Circle the word that is spelled correctly.

walk   walc   walck

NAME: _____

DIRECTIONS Read and answer each question.

1. Write the name of your favorite month.

_____

– – – – – – – – – – – – – – – –

_____

1. Ⓨ Ⓝ

2. Ⓨ Ⓝ

2. Add commas.

We all need water food and air to live.

3. Ⓨ Ⓝ

4. Ⓨ Ⓝ

___/ 4
Total

3. Write the adjective.

The _____ party was fun.
      (hair or **nice)**

4. Write the correct word.

The sign says to _____.
                  (stop or **step)**

NAME: _____

1. Ⓨ Ⓝ

2. Ⓨ Ⓝ

3. Ⓨ Ⓝ

4. Ⓨ Ⓝ

___/4
Total

DIRECTIONS Read and answer each question.

1. Which word needs a capital letter? Write it correctly on the line.

Jan and brett are friends.

_____

- - - - - - - - - - - - - - - - - - -

_____

2. Add a comma.

Is our vacation on

May 13 2016?

3. Write the correct pronoun.

_____
- - - -
_____ open the door to go inside.
(Me or **I)**

4. Write the correct word.

_____
A - - - - - - - means you are happy.
(grin or **grip)**

NAME: _____

DIRECTIONS   Read and answer each question.

1. Add a name to the sentence.

I go to _____ 's house.

2. Add punctuation.

Today is Monday

3. Circle the pronoun.

Joe likes his pet, Rex.

4. Circle the word that is spelled correctly.

zew   zu   zoo

NAME: _____

DIRECTIONS Read and answer each question.

1. Circle the words that need capital letters.

Do we go on may 4 or june 4?

2. Add a comma.

It will be January 6 2016 soon.

3. Write the present tense verb.

The dog _____ at the park.
(**ran** or **runs**)

4. Write the correct word.

The dog must _____.
(**set** or **sit**)

NAME: _____

DIRECTIONS Read and answer each question.

SCORE

1. Add a name to the sentence.

I live close to _____.

1. Ⓨ Ⓝ

2. Ⓨ Ⓝ

2. Add punctuation.

Who needs a pen

3. Ⓨ Ⓝ

4. Ⓨ Ⓝ

3. Write the past tense verb.

The fish _____.

(**moved** or **moves**)

___/4
Total

4. Circle the word that is spelled correctly.

room   roum   reum

NAME: _____

DIRECTIONS Read and answer each question.

1. Circle the words that need capital letters.

1. Ⓨ Ⓝ

Is june or july coming up next?

2. Ⓨ Ⓝ

2. Write a date that is special to you. Include a comma.

3. Ⓨ Ⓝ

_____

4. Ⓨ Ⓝ

— — — — — — — — — — — — — — — —

_____

___ / 4
Total

3. Write the correct pronoun.

_____

I see _____ at home.
      (**him** or **he**)

4. Write the correct word.

_____

I am _____ friend.
     (**has** or **his**)

NAME: _____

DIRECTIONS Read and answer each question.

1. Add a name to the sentence.

I like to read with _____.

2. Add punctuation.

You are very funny

3. Write the correct noun.

The fastest _____ wins.

(**runner** or **runners**)

4. Circle the word that is spelled correctly.

soon   sown   suen

NAME: _____

SCORE

1. Ⓨ Ⓝ

2. Ⓨ Ⓝ

3. Ⓨ Ⓝ

4. Ⓨ Ⓝ

___/ 4
Total

DIRECTIONS Read and answer each question.

1. Add a name to the sentence.

I am older than _____.

2. Add commas.

Our flag is red white and blue.

3. Write the adjective.

The _____ tree is growing.
(**small** or **leaf**)

4. Write the correct word.

The girls _____ to play.
(**ran** or **rat**)

NAME: _____

DIRECTIONS Read and answer each question.

1. Add the day of the week.

Tomorrow will be _____.

1. Ⓨ Ⓝ

2. Add commas.

Let's play with a ball a bat and a mitt.

2. Ⓨ Ⓝ

3. Ⓨ Ⓝ

4. Ⓨ Ⓝ

___ / 4
Total

3. Write the present tense verb.

Our dog _____ on the beach.
       (ran or **runs)**

4. Circle the word that is spelled correctly.

bocks   boxe   box

NAME: _____

DIRECTIONS Read and answer each question.

1. Add a name to the sentence.

I am taller than _____.

2. Add a comma.

The game will be on June 4 2016.

3. Circle the pronoun.

Paula misses her friend.

4. Write the correct word.

Who _____ the book first?
(**had** or **ham**)

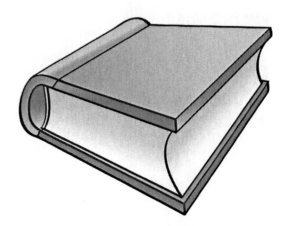

NAME: _____

DIRECTIONS Read and answer each question.

1. Circle the word that needs a capital letter.

Our next school holiday is in october.

2. Add a comma.

January 15 2016 will be a special day.

3. Write the correct noun.

The _____ is blue.
(**car** or **cars**)

4. Write the correct word.

The _____ may be very hot.
(**pot** or **rot**)

NAME: _____

SCORE

1. Ⓨ Ⓝ

2. Ⓨ Ⓝ

3. Ⓨ Ⓝ

4. Ⓨ Ⓝ

___ / 4
Total

DIRECTIONS Read and answer each question.

1. Add a name to the sentence.

I am younger than _____.

2. Add commas.

I asked my mom for cheese

bananas and crackers for lunch.

3. Write the correct verb.

The waves _____ on the sand.

(**crash** or **crashes**)

4. Circle the word that is spelled correctly.

such   sutch   sucht

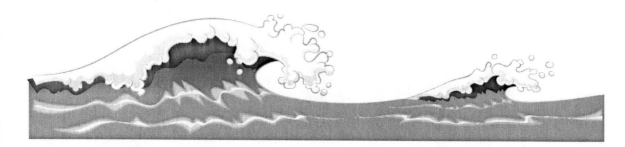

NAME: _____

DIRECTIONS Read and answer each question.

1. Add a name to the sentence.

Yesterday, I played with

_____

— — — — — — — — — — — — — — — — — —

_____ .

2. Add punctuation.

The dog loves to walk

3. Write the past tense verb.

The dog _____ the grass.
(smells or smelled)

4. Circle the word that is spelled correctly.

boan   bown   bone

NAME: _____

SCORE

DIRECTIONS Read and answer each question.

1. Y N

2. Y N

3. Y N

4. Y N

___ / 4
Total

1. Add a name to the sentence.

Yesterday, I read to

_____

– – – – – – – – – – – – – –

_____ .

2. Add commas.

Ted has red purple and

blue crayons.

3. Write the correct word.

The ball lands in _____ bush.
(**a** or **an**)

4. Circle the word that is spelled correctly.

keap   keep   kepe

NAME: _____

DIRECTIONS Read and answer each question.

1. Add a name to the sentence.

Yesterday, I talked with
_____

- - - - - - - - - - - - - - - - - -

_____ .

2. Add punctuation.

Who wants to be my partner

3. Write the correct pronoun.

My mom told _____ to be safe.
(me or **my)**

4. Write the correct word.

Let's play with _____ !
(them or **then)**

NAME: _____

DIRECTIONS Read and answer each question.

1. Add a name to the sentence.

_____

_ _ _ _ _ _ _ _ _ _ _ _ _

_____ is nice.

2. Add commas.

The bus driver told us to keep arms legs and heads inside.

3. Circle the nouns.

The ball flew over the net.

4. Circle the word that is spelled correctly.

push   poosh   poush

#51166—180 Days of Language

NAME: _____

DIRECTIONS Read and answer each question.

1. Add a name to the sentence.

_____

— — — — — — — — helps me stay healthy.

2. Add punctuation.

That yelling is way too loud

3. Write the correct noun.

The — — — — — — — — growl.
  (**tiger** or **tigers**)

4. Write the correct word.

— — — — — — — — — — are you going?
  (**Were** or **Where**)

NAME: _____

DIRECTIONS Read and answer each question.

SCORE

1. Ⓨ Ⓝ

2. Ⓨ Ⓝ

3. Ⓨ Ⓝ

4. Ⓨ Ⓝ

___ / 4
Total

1. Write the name of your favorite day of the week.

_____

- - - - - - - - - - - - - - - -

_____

2. Add a comma.

Leap Day is on
February 29 2016.

3. Circle the adjectives.

There are yummy treats at
surprise parties.

4. Write the correct word.

Please put the cup _____.

(**her** or **here**)

NAME: _____

DIRECTIONS   Read and answer each question.

1. Name a cold month.

_____

- - - - - - - - - - - - - - - - - -

_____

2. Add punctuation.

How did you get to school

3. Write the adjective

Sam is _____.

(**boy** or **sweet**)

4. Write a word with the *-ack* pattern as in *back*.

_____

- -

_____

NAME: _____

1. Ⓨ Ⓝ

2. Ⓨ Ⓝ

3. Ⓨ Ⓝ

4. Ⓨ Ⓝ

___ / 4
Total

DIRECTIONS Read and answer each question.

1. Name a warm month.

_____

_ _ _ _ _ _ _ _ _ _ _ _ _

_____

2. Add a comma.

What will we do on
January 4 2016?

3. Write the correct noun.

The _____ was very fast.
(**sled** or **sleds**)

4. Write the correct word.

The cat is _____ the fence.
(**by** or **buy**)

NAME: _____

DIRECTIONS Read and answer each question.

1. Name the month we are in.

_____

_ _ _ _ _ _ _ _ _ _ _ _ _ _

_____

2. Add punctuation.

This math game is fun

3. Circle the verb.

I rode past the park.

4. Write a word with the *-ick* pattern as in *pick*.

_____

_ _ _ _ _ _ _ _ _ _ _ _ _ _

_____

NAME: _____

1. (Y)(N)

2. (Y)(N)

3. (Y)(N)

4. (Y)(N)

___ / 4
Total

DIRECTIONS Read and answer each question.

1. Write the name of last month.

_____

- - - - - - - - - - - - - - - -

_____

2. Add commas.

The cafeteria has milk water and juice.

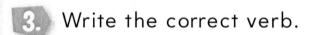

3. Write the correct verb.

The bunny _____ away.

(**hop** or **hops**)

4. Write a word with the -ack pattern as in tack.

_____

- - - - - - - - - - - - - - - -

_____

 #51166—180 Days of Language

NAME: _____

DIRECTIONS Read and answer each question.

1. What is tomorrow's date?

_____

— — — — — — — — — — — —

_____

2. Add punctuation.

Where is my lunch

3. Circle the pronoun.

Yesterday, I ate a salad.

4. Write a word with the *-at* pattern as in *rat*.

_____

— — — — — — — — — — — —

_____

NAME: _____

DIRECTIONS Read and answer each question.

1. (Y)(N)

1. Circle the words that need capital letters.

today, i want to go to the movies.

2. (Y)(N)

2. Add a comma.

3. (Y)(N)

Where will you be on

May 5 2016?

4. (Y)(N)

___ / 4
Total

3. Write the adjective.

My _____ dog does not like to run.
   (**old** or **ear**)

4. Write a word with the -op pattern as in top.

_____

_ _ _ _ _ _ _ _ _ _ _ _ _ _ _

_____

#51166—180 Days of Language

NAME: _____

DIRECTIONS Read and answer each question.

SCORE

1. Circle the word that needs a capital letter.

I will ask mrs. Jones a question.

1. Ⓨ Ⓝ

2. Ⓨ Ⓝ

2. Add punctuation.

I am very excited for the sleepover

3. Ⓨ Ⓝ

4. Ⓨ Ⓝ

3. Write the correct verb.

How did you _____?

(**feels** or **feel**)

___/ 4
Total

4. Write a word with the *-ing* pattern as in *ring*.

_____

__ __ __ __ __ __ __ __ __ __ __ __ __ __

NAME: _____

DIRECTIONS Read and answer each question.

1. Rewrite the sentence using correct capitalization.

I am going on a trip in july.

_____
- - - - - - - - - - - - - - - - -
_____
- - - - - - - - - - - - - - - - -
_____

2. Add commas.

I ate rice beans and salsa

for dinner.

3. Write the adjective.

                                    _____
                                    - - - - - - - -
The band played _____ music.
                    (**drums** or **loud**)

4. Circle the word that is spelled correctly.

evry   evre   every

NAME: _____

DIRECTIONS   Read and answer each question.

1.   Write a sentence using at least one capital letter.

_____

— — — — — — — — — — — — — — —

_____

_____

— — — — — — — — — — — — — — —

_____

1. Ⓨ Ⓝ

2. Ⓨ Ⓝ

3. Ⓨ Ⓝ

2.   Add punctuation.

My party is on March 3 2015.

4. Ⓨ Ⓝ

___ / 4
Total

3.   Circle the pronouns.

I did not see the boy until he

ran out.

4.   Circle the word that is spelled correctly.

rownd   round   rowned

NAME: _____

DIRECTIONS Read and answer each question.

1. Ⓨ Ⓝ

2. Ⓨ Ⓝ

3. Ⓨ Ⓝ

4. Ⓨ Ⓝ

___/ 4
Total

1. What is the day after February 20?

_____

- - - - - - - - - - - - - - - -

_____

2. Add punctuation.

Where is our teacher

3. Circle the adjectives.

Pam loves small, blue birds.

4. Write the correct word.

Sam wants _____ food.

(**some** or **sum**)

 #51166—180 Days of Language

NAME: _____

DIRECTIONS Read and answer each question.

1. What is the day before March 15?

_____

_ _

_____

1. Ⓨ Ⓝ

2. Ⓨ Ⓝ

2. What is one year after October 14, 2014?

_____

_ _

_____

3. Ⓨ Ⓝ

4. Ⓨ Ⓝ

___ / 4
Total

3. Write the present tense verb.

_____

Kai _ _ _ _ _ _ _ _ _ _ outside.
      (**stepped** or **steps**)

4. Write the correct word.

_____

The _ _ _ _ _ _ _ _ _ _ of a horse lasts

      (**live** or **life**)

many years.

NAME: _____

DIRECTIONS Read and answer each question.

SCORE

1. Ⓨ Ⓝ

2. Ⓨ Ⓝ

3. Ⓨ Ⓝ

4. Ⓨ Ⓝ

___ / 4
Total

1. What is the day after April 20?

_____

- - - - - - - - - - - - - - - -

_____

2. Add punctuation.

The pig slept in the sun

3. Combine these two sentences. Include a comma and the word *or*.

Chloe eats ice cream. She eats

cake.

_____

- - - - - - - - - - - - - - - -

_____

- - - - - - - - - - - - - - - -

_____

4. Write the correct word.

When will we _____?

(**know** or **now**)

NAME: _____

DIRECTIONS Read and answer each question.

1. What is the day after July 4?

_____

- - - - - - - - - - - - - - - - - -

_____

2. What is one year before May 9, 2017?

_____

- - - - - - - - - - - - - - - - - -

_____

3. Combine these two sentences. Include a comma and the word *but.*

Evan had practice. He didn't

want to go.

_____

- - - - - - - - - - - - - - - - - -

_____

- - - - - - - - - - - - - - - - - -

_____

4. Circle the word that is spelled correctly.

walk   wallk   wak

NAME: _____

DIRECTIONS   Read and answer each question.

1. What is the day before October 2?

_____

- - - - - - - - - - - -

_____

2. Add punctuation.

Who can water

the garden

3. Write the correct verb.

The spider _____ on the web.

(**move** or **moves**)

4. Write a word with the -*it* pattern as in *bit*.

_____

- - - - - - - - - - - -

_____

NAME: _____

DIRECTIONS Read and answer each question.

1. Circle the word that needs a capital letter.

I want to play with ernie.

1. Ⓨ Ⓝ

2. Ⓨ Ⓝ

2. Add punctuation.

When will school start

3. Ⓨ Ⓝ

3. Write the correct noun.

_____

_____ sister went to bed.
(**Avas** or **Ava's**)

4. Ⓨ Ⓝ

___/ 4
Total

4. Write the correct word.

Can you spot the _____ ?
(**bat** or **bhat**)

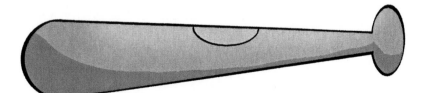

NAME: _____

DIRECTIONS Read and answer each question.

1. Circle the words that need capital letters.

mr. evans wants to see me.

2. Add punctuation.

The bunny hopped away

3. Write the correct pronoun.

Pam left, but _____ forgot
_ _ _ _ _ _
(**her** or **she**)

her lunch.

4. Write a word with the -ot pattern as in *hot*.

_____

_ _ _ _ _ _ _ _ _ _ _ _ _ _ _ _ _

 #51166—180 Days of Language

NAME: _____

DIRECTIONS Read and answer each question.

1. Circle the word that needs a capital letter.

The teacher told nico to get to work.

2. Add a comma.

Mark the calendar for October 25 2016.

3. Write the correct subject.

_____ _____

_____ _____ feeds the cows.

(**The farmers** or **The farmer**)

4. Circle the word that is spelled correctly.

please   pleez   plese

1. Ⓨ Ⓝ

2. Ⓨ Ⓝ

3. Ⓨ Ⓝ

4. Ⓨ Ⓝ

___ / 4
Total

NAME: _____

SCORE

DIRECTIONS Read and answer each question.

1. Y N

1. Circle the word that needs a capital letter.

My coach, brad, was not happy today.

2. Y N

2. Add commas.

The band played drums piano and guitar.

3. Y N

4. Y N

3. Write the correct noun.

_____

___ ___ ___ ___ ___ ___ coat was nice.

___ / 4
Total

(**Ruby's** or **Rubys**)

4. Write a word with the -et pattern as in *met*.

_____

___ ___ ___ ___ ___ ___ ___ ___

 #51166—180 Days of Language

NAME: _____

Read and answer each question.

SCORE

1. Circle the word that needs a capital letter.

When will ella be able to play?

1. Ⓨ Ⓝ

2. Ⓨ Ⓝ

2. Add commas.

The plant was tall green and healthy.

3. Ⓨ Ⓝ

4. Ⓨ Ⓝ

___ / 4
Total

3. Write the past tense verb.

The animals _____ the train.
(**moved** or **move**)

4. Circle the word that is spelled correctly.

have   hav   halv

NAME: _____

SCORE

1. Y N

2. Y N

3. Y N

4. Y N

___ / 4
Total

1. Circle the word that needs a capital letter.

My mom has a birthday on may 2.

2. Add commas.

Chloe is tall smart and kind.

3. What is another way to write *the nest in the tree?*

the tree nest

the trees' nest

the tree's nest

4. Write the correct word.

Please do not get _____.

(**hunt** or **hurt**)

NAME: _____

DIRECTIONS Read and answer each question.

1. Circle the word that needs a capital letter.

My dad comes home on july 24.

2. Add commas.

Jake's car was red
shiny and fast.

3. Circle the nouns.

The chair is beside the desk.

4. Write a word with the -*ug* pattern as in *hug*.

_____

- - - - - - - - - - - - - - - -

_____

NAME: _____

DIRECTIONS   Read and answer each question.

SCORE

1. Ⓨ Ⓝ

2. Ⓨ Ⓝ

3. Ⓨ Ⓝ

4. Ⓨ Ⓝ

___ / 4
Total

1. Circle the word that needs a capital letter.

Can cole stack the toys for me?

2. Add commas.

The cookies had sugar salt and flour.

3. Add a pronoun.

_____ played in the backyard all day.

4. Write the correct word.

Marco can _____ the ball
(**toss** or **toes**)
to Sid.

NAME: _____

DIRECTIONS Read and answer each question.

1. Circle the word that needs a capital letter.

When will olivia be home?

2. What is another way to say *the hat on Faith*?

Faiths hat

Faithes hat

Faith's hat

3. Write an adjective.

The singer sang a _____

song.

4. Write a word with the *-un* pattern as in *sun*.

_____

NAME: _____

Read and answer each question.

SCORE

1. Ⓨ Ⓝ

2. Ⓨ Ⓝ

3. Ⓨ Ⓝ

4. Ⓨ Ⓝ

___ / 4
Total

1. Circle the word that needs a capital letter.

Why did liam have to go home?

2. Add an apostrophe.

the teachers book

3. Combine the two sentences. Include a comma and the word *or*.

Sally can go to the pool. She can go to the park.

_____

- - - - - - - - - - - - - - - -

_____

- - - - - - - - - - - - - - - -

_____

4. Write the correct word.

Make sure to wash the _____.

(**pan** or **pat**)

NAME: _____

DIRECTIONS Read and answer each question.

1. Circle the word that needs a capital letter.

Why is milo mad at me?

1. Ⓨ Ⓝ

2. Add punctuation.

Karen saw a bug in her room

2. Ⓨ Ⓝ

3. Ⓨ Ⓝ

3. Combine the two sentences. Include a comma and the word *but*.

4. Ⓨ Ⓝ

Iris had to do her homework. She

ate first.

___/ 4
Total

_____
_ _ _ _ _ _ _ _ _ _ _ _ _ _ _ _
_____
_ _ _ _ _ _ _ _ _ _ _ _ _ _ _ _
_____

4. Write a word with the *-ig* pattern as in *rig*.

_____
_ _ _ _ _ _ _ _ _ _ _ _ _ _ _ _
_____

NAME: _____

DIRECTIONS Read and answer each question.

SCORE

1. Ⓨ Ⓝ

2. Ⓨ Ⓝ

3. Ⓨ Ⓝ

4. Ⓨ Ⓝ

___ / 4
Total

1. Circle the words that need capital letters.

I know that dr. fisher is very kind.

2. Add a comma.

I turn 10 on January 29 2019.

3. Use an apostrophe to write *the sister of Sara* in another way.

_____

_____

4. Write a word with the *-ea* pattern as in *beach*.

_____

_____

NAME: _____

Read and answer each question.

1. Circle the words that need capital letters.

I have to see dr. baxter tomorrow.

2. Add punctuation.

Who is in the car

3. Add an apostrophe.

Lilas teacher was gone on Friday.

4. Write a word with the *-et* pattern as in *pet*.

_____

_ _ _ _ _ _ _ _ _ _ _ _ _ _

_____

SCORE

1. Ⓨ Ⓝ

2. Ⓨ Ⓝ

3. Ⓨ Ⓝ

4. Ⓨ Ⓝ

___ / 4
Total

NAME: _____

1. (Y)(N)

2. (Y)(N)

3. (Y)(N)

4. (Y)(N)

___ / 4
Total

DIRECTIONS Read and answer each question.

1. Circle the words that need capital letters.

I think that mrs. harris is a great teacher.

2. Add punctuation.

Watch out for the rock

3. Circle the pronoun.

Dan likes to ride his bike.

4. Circle the word that is spelled correctly.

pash   path   pathe

NAME: _____

DIRECTIONS Read and answer each question.

1. Circle the words that need capital letters.

Our team likes coach sandy.

2. Add punctuation.

I think you should go home

3. Add an adjective.

My friend is _____.

4. Write a word with the *-ow* pattern as in *cow*.

_____

_____

NAME: _____

DIRECTIONS Read and answer each question.

1. Circle the word that needs a capital letter.

I need help with my homework from jamie.

2. Add punctuation.

Do you think I can do that

3. Write the correct verb.

Carter did not _____ well.
(**feel** or **feels**)

4. Circle the word that is spelled correctly.

fuir   fer   fur

NAME: _____

DIRECTIONS Read and answer each question.

1. Circle the words that need capital letters.

1. Ⓨ Ⓝ

Our principal is mrs. sanchez.

2. Ⓨ Ⓝ

2. Add punctuation.

3. Ⓨ Ⓝ

Do not let go of the rope

4. Ⓨ Ⓝ

3. Which is another way to write *the game belonging to Juan*?

___/4
Total

Juan's game

Juanes game

Juans game

4. Which word is **not** spelled correctly?

fast   fist   fost

NAME: _____

SCORE

1. Ⓨ Ⓝ

2. Ⓨ Ⓝ

3. Ⓨ Ⓝ

4. Ⓨ Ⓝ

___ / 4
Total

DIRECTIONS Read and answer each question.

1. Circle the words that need capital letters.

The first grade teachers are mrs. johns and mr. paulson.

2. Add punctuation.

I am hungry

3. Write the past tense verb.

The artist _____ a painting.
(**makes** or **made**)

4. Which word is **not** spelled correctly?

rack   rhuck   rock

NAME: _____

DIRECTIONS   Read and answer each question.

1. Circle the words that need capital letters.

abby and max are good friends.

2. Add punctuation.

Why are you mad

3. Circle the pronoun.

Kara and I walked to school.

4. Which word is **not** spelled correctly?

top   tep   tip

NAME: _____

DIRECTIONS Read and answer each question.

SCORE

1. (Y)(N)

2. (Y)(N)

3. (Y)(N)

4. (Y)(N)

___/4
Total

1. Circle the word that needs a capital letter.

I hope that jake can fix my bike.

2. Add the correct punctuation.

I cannot wait for recess

3. Write the correct verb.

The sisters _____ over
(**argue** or **argues**)

the game.

4. Circle the word that is spelled correctly.

owr   our   ouer

NAME: _____

Read and answer each question.

1. Circle the word that needs a capital letter.

I want nate to come over.

2. Add punctuation.

How will I get that done

3. Write the present tense verb.

I _____ my milk into
(**poured** or **pour**)

the glass.

4. Write the correct word.

The pool is too _____.
(**deep** or **keep**)

NAME: _____

DIRECTIONS Read and answer each question.

1. Y N

1. What is the day after October 5?

_____

‑ ‑ ‑ ‑ ‑ ‑ ‑ ‑ ‑ ‑ ‑ ‑ ‑ ‑ ‑ ‑ ‑

_____

2. Y N

3. Y N

2. Add punctuation.

That is very scary

4. Y N

____/ 4
Total

3. Circle the pronoun.

We are such good friends.

4. Which word is **not** spelled correctly?

gap   tap   fap

NAME: _____

DIRECTIONS Read and answer each question.

1. Circle the word that needs a capital letter.

My mom is named lily.

1. Ⓨ Ⓝ

2. Add punctuation.

The sunset at the beach

was pretty

2. Ⓨ Ⓝ

3. Ⓨ Ⓝ

4. Ⓨ Ⓝ

___ / 4
Total

3. Add an apostrophe.

Ninas art was hung on the wall.

4. Write the correct word.

It is my job to _____ our cat.
(feed or **feel)**

NAME: _____

SCORE

1. Ⓨ Ⓝ

2. Ⓨ Ⓝ

3. Ⓨ Ⓝ

4. Ⓨ Ⓝ

___ / 4
Total

1. Circle the word that needs a capital letter.

Save the treat for april 2.

2. Add punctuation.

The plant needs water and sun

3. Write an adjective.

Going to a pool is fun on a

_____ day.

4. Which word is **not** spelled correctly?

sip   sep   sap

NAME: _____

DIRECTIONS Read and answer each question.

1. Circle the word that needs a capital letter.

My sister ann wants a snack.

2. Add punctuation.

Where is my glass

3. Circle the nouns.

The dog and cat like to play.

4. Write the correct word.

She _____ to bed after
(**cane** or **came**)

the show.

NAME: _____

SCORE

DIRECTIONS   Read and answer each question.

1. Add a name to the sentence.

1. Ⓨ Ⓝ

I talked to _____ today.

2. Ⓨ Ⓝ

3. Ⓨ Ⓝ

2. Add punctuation.

Who can come over today

4. Ⓨ Ⓝ

___ / 4
Total

3. Write the correct verb.

The baby _____ when he
(**cry** or **cries**)

is tired.

4. Circle the word that is spelled correctly.

very   verry   vairy

NAME: _____

DIRECTIONS Read and answer each question.

1. Add a name to the sentence.

I like to eat lunch with

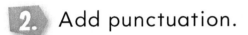

_____

_ _ _ _ _ _ _ _ _ _ _ _ _ _

_____ .

1. Ⓨ Ⓝ

2. Ⓨ Ⓝ

2. Add punctuation.

I am feeling very happy

3. Ⓨ Ⓝ

4. Ⓨ Ⓝ

___ / 4
Total

3. Circle the pronoun.

Parker thought he heard a noise.

4. Write the correct word.

Dad _____ his bike to work.
(rod or **rode)**

NAME: _____

DIRECTIONS Read and answer each question.

1. Add a name to the sentence.

A friend in this class is
_____
_ _ _ _ _ _ _ _ _ _ _ _ _ _ _
_____.

2. Add commas.

The cake had red pink and
blue frosting.

3. Write the correct verb.

Claire _____ in the pool.
(**swims** or **swim**)

4. Circle the word that is spelled correctly.

because   becuz   beecause

NAME: _____

DIRECTIONS Read and answer each question.

1. Add a name to the sentence.

A friend in another class is

_____

_ _ _ _ _ _ _ _ _ _ _ _ _ _

_____ .

2. Add commas.

My mom made rice chicken

and carrots.

3. Circle the possessive noun.

My friend's mom is nice.

4. Write the correct word.

Juan can _____ on one foot.

(**hop** or **hope**)

NAME: _____

1. Ⓨ Ⓝ

2. Ⓨ Ⓝ

3. Ⓨ Ⓝ

4. Ⓨ Ⓝ

___ / 4
Total

DIRECTIONS Read and answer each question.

1. Add a name to the sentence.

An older friend of mine is

_____

– – – – – – – – – – – – –

_____ .

2. Add commas.

We need glue paper and scissors for the project.

3. Circle the verb.

Jack's dad took us to school.

4. Write a word with the *-op* pattern as in *stop*.

_____

– – – – – – – – – – – – –

_____

 #51166—180 Days of Language

NAME: _____

DIRECTIONS Read and answer each question.

1. Add a name to the sentence.

A younger friend is
_ _ _ _ _ _ _ _ _ _ _ _ _ _ _ _ _
_____.

2. Add commas.

The book has action suspense
and mystery.

3. Write the past tense verb.

The kids _____ to ride bikes.
(**liked** or **likes**)

4. Write the correct word.

Dad cooks in a _____.
(**pan** or **pat**)

NAME: _____

DIRECTIONS Read and answer each question.

1. Circle the word that needs a capital letter.

Don't forget to come on july 24.

2. Add commas.

Please bring water a ball and a snack to practice.

3. Write the correct verb.

Our choir _____ in the show.

(**sing** or **sings**)

4. Circle the word that is spelled correctly.

goeing   gowing   going

NAME: _____

Read and answer each question.

1. Circle the word that needs a capital letter.

Tomorrow will be august 3.

1. Ⓨ Ⓝ

2. Ⓨ Ⓝ

2. Add a comma.

The big game will be on June 5 2015.

3. Ⓨ Ⓝ

4. Ⓨ Ⓝ

___ / 4
Total

3. Write the present tense verb.

The teachers _____

(**decided** or **decide**)

to give a test.

4. Write a word with the -*all* pattern as in *call*.

_____

- - - - - - - - - - - -
_____

DAY
139

NAME: ____________________

DIRECTIONS Read and answer each question.

SCORE

1. Ⓨ Ⓝ

2. Ⓨ Ⓝ

3. Ⓨ Ⓝ

4. Ⓨ Ⓝ

___ / 4
Total

1. What is the day after March 9?

____

2. Add a comma.

We have to move on

May 15 2016.

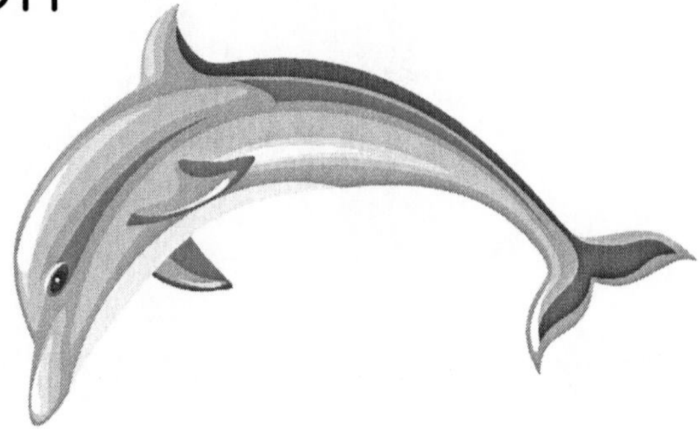

3. Circle the nouns.

The scientists see the dolphins.

4. Circle the word that is spelled correctly.

once   wonce   wons

NAME: _____

DIRECTIONS Read and answer each question.

1. What is the day before December 2?

_____

_ _ _ _ _ _ _ _ _ _ _ _ _ _ _ _ _ _

_____

2. Add a comma.

Our school closes on June 15 2014.

3. Write two adjectives about cafeteria food.

_____

_ _ _ _ _ _ _ _ _ _ _ _ _ _ _ _ _

_____

_____

_ _ _ _ _ _ _ _ _ _ _ _ _ _ _ _ _

_____

4. Write a word with the -*ast* pattern as in *fast*.

_____

_ _ _ _ _ _ _ _ _ _ _ _ _ _ _ _ _

_____

NAME: _____

DIRECTIONS Read and answer each question.

1. What is a date that is special to you?

_____

- - - - - - - - - - - - - - - - - -

_____

2. Add punctuation.

Can you fix the window

3. Write the present tense verb.

The rain _____.

(**stopped** or **stops**)

4. Add an *-ing* ending to the base word *eat*.

_____

- - - - - - - - - - - - - - - - - -

_____

NAME: _____

DIRECTIONS Read and answer each question.

1. Circle the words that need capital letters.

I had lunch with grandpa bill and grandma maria.

2. Add punctuation.

Do you like to eat vegetables

3. Write the correct noun.

Please get your _____
(**work** or **works**)

done soon.

4. Which word is **not** spelled correctly?

hear   here   heer

NAME: _____

SCORE

DIRECTIONS Read and answer each question.

1. Write the name of a family member.

_____

- - - - - - - - - - - - - - - - - -

_____

1. Ⓨ Ⓝ

2. Ⓨ Ⓝ

3. Ⓨ Ⓝ

4. Ⓨ Ⓝ

___ / 4
Total

2. Add a comma.

The calendar stops on

December 31 2015.

3. Write the correct verb.

The baby _____ his mother.

(**find** or **finds**)

4. Which word is **not** spelled correctly?

tail   tael   tale

NAME: _____

DIRECTIONS   Read and answer each question.

1. Which kinds of words are always capitalized?

months   verbs   nouns

2. Add commas.

There are ants spiders and other bugs outside.

3. Write the past tense verb.

Sylvia _____ her dog.
      (walks or **walked)**

4. Which word is **not** spelled correctly?

ower   hour   our

NAME: _____

Read and answer each question.

SCORE

1. Ⓨ Ⓝ

2. Ⓨ Ⓝ

3. Ⓨ Ⓝ

4. Ⓨ Ⓝ

___ / 4
Total

1. Add a name to the sentence.

I want to work with

_____

_ _ _ _ _ _ _ _ _ _ _ _

_____ today.

2. Add commas.

We need fans water and ice

to stay cool.

3. Combine the two sentences. Include the word *and*.

I can have pizza. I can have milk.

_____

_ _ _ _ _ _ _ _ _ _ _ _

_____

_ _ _ _ _ _ _ _ _ _ _ _

_____

4. Which word is **not** spelled correctly?

meet   meat   meit

NAME: _____

DIRECTIONS Read and answer each question.

1. Circle the words that need capital letters.

Both uncle bob and uncle carlos came to my party.

1. Ⓨ Ⓝ

2. Ⓨ Ⓝ

2. Add punctuation.

The hive was buzzing

3. Ⓨ Ⓝ

4. Ⓨ Ⓝ

___ / 4
Total

3. Write the past tense verb.

Chris _____ a cake.
       (**bakes** or **baked**)

4. Which spelling pattern makes a word that starts with *fl-*?

−at   −et   −en

NAME: _____

SCORE

1. Ⓨ Ⓝ

2. Ⓨ Ⓝ

3. Ⓨ Ⓝ

4. Ⓨ Ⓝ

___ / 4
Total

1. Add a name to the sentence.

I want to play with

_____

_ _ _ _ _ _ _ _ _ _ _ _ _ _ _

_____ today.

2. Add punctuation.

Why does this always happen

3. Use an apostrophe to write *the lunch box of Kara* in another way.

_____

_ _

_____

4. Which spelling pattern makes a word that starts with *st-*?

–ep   –er   –en

NAME: _____

DIRECTIONS Read and answer each question.

1. Circle the words that need capital letters.

Is our field trip on may 4 or june 4?

2. Add punctuation.

The beach was very dirty

3. Circle the adjectives.

Cheesy pizza is delicious.

4. Which spelling pattern makes a word that starts with *dr-*?

-ot   -op   -om

NAME: _____

DIRECTIONS Read and answer each question.

1. Add a name to the sentence.

I want to read with

_____

— — — — — — — — — —
_____ today.

2. Add punctuation.

How can we get home

3. Write the correct verb.

_____
The lions — — — — — — — very fast.
(**run** or **runs**)

4. Which spelling pattern makes a word that starts with *sl-*?

–an   –ad   –ab

NAME: _____

DIRECTIONS Read and answer each question.

1. Circle the word that needs a capital letter.

The play will be on may 4.

2. Add punctuation.

This is the best day ever

3. Add an apostrophe.

Kevins aunt took care of me.

4. Which spelling pattern makes a word that starts with *cl-*?

-al   -ep   -ap

NAME: _____

DIRECTIONS Read and answer each question.

1. Add a name to the sentence.

_____

I read with ─ ─ ─ ─ ─ ─ ─ ─

today.

2. Add punctuation.

Who is your teacher

3. Write a sentence using the word *except.*

_____
─ ─ ─ ─ ─ ─ ─ ─ ─ ─ ─ ─ ─ ─
_____
─ ─ ─ ─ ─ ─ ─ ─ ─ ─ ─ ─ ─ ─
_____

4. Which spelling pattern makes a word that starts with *pl-?*

–an   –ad   –ap

NAME: _____

DIRECTIONS Read and answer each question.

1. Add a name to the sentence.

My friend _____
is wearing blue.

2. Add punctuation.

The car zoomed by

3. Circle the pronoun.

Zia asked to have her friends over.

4. Which spelling pattern makes a word that starts with *tr-*?

−in   −id   −ip

NAME: _____

DIRECTIONS Read and answer each question.

1. Add a name to the sentence.

I will see _____

today.

2. Add punctuation.

Where is your house

3. Write the correct noun.

The _____ work very hard.

(**cop** or **cops**)

4. Which spelling pattern makes a word that starts
with *sl-*?

‾oc   ‾ug   ‾on

NAME: _____

DIRECTIONS Read and answer each question.

1. Add a name to the sentence.

My friend _____

makes me laugh.

2. Add commas.

The story had characters named Fred Ted and Ned.

3. What is another way to write *the time machine of the scientist*?

_____

_____

_____

4. Which spelling pattern makes a word that starts with *gr-*?

–in   –od   –ap

NAME: _____

SCORE

1. Ⓨ Ⓝ

2. Ⓨ Ⓝ

3. Ⓨ Ⓝ

4. Ⓨ Ⓝ

___ / 4
Total

DIRECTIONS Read and answer each question.

1. Add a name to the sentence.

I will see _____ today.

2. Add commas.

I want to go home go to the pool and go to the park.

3. Circle the nouns.

The boat came to shore.

4. Which spelling pattern makes a word that starts with *cl*-?

–in   –id   –ip

NAME: _____

DIRECTIONS Read and answer each question.

1. Circle the words that need capital letters.

I have to see dr. walker and dr. martinez about my broken arm.

2. Write today's date. Include a comma.

_____

_ _ _ _ _ _ _ _ _ _ _ _ _ _ _ _ _ _

_____

3. Write the correct pronoun.

Pablo loves to play with

_____

_ _ _ _ _ _ _ _ brother.

(**their** or **his**)

4. Unscramble the middle letters to make a word.

_____

c a l p _ _ _ _ _ _ _ _ _ _ _

NAME: _____

SCORE

1. Ⓨ Ⓝ

2. Ⓨ Ⓝ

3. Ⓨ Ⓝ

4. Ⓨ Ⓝ

___ / 4
Total

DIRECTIONS Read and answer each question.

1. Add a name to the sentence.

I will see _____ today.

2. Write tomorrow's date. Include a comma.

_____

- -

_____

3. Circle the verb.

A car drives by the store.

4. Unscramble the middle letters to make a word.

c n o e _____

#51166—180 Days of Language

NAME: _____

DIRECTIONS Read and answer each question.

1. Write a sentence about a special date.

_____
_ _ _ _ _ _ _ _ _ _ _ _ _ _ _ _ _ _
_____
_ _ _ _ _ _ _ _ _ _ _ _ _ _ _ _ _ _
_____

2. Add punctuation.

I will go to the park

3. Write the correct verb.

The band _____.
_ _ _ _ _ _ _ _ _ _
(travel or **travels)**

4. Unscramble the middle letters to make a word.

p a l y _____
_ _ _ _ _ _ _ _ _ _ _ _ _

NAME: _____

SCORE

DIRECTIONS Read and answer each question.

1. Y N

1. Add a name to the sentence.

_____

I hope that _____

helps me today.

2. Y N

3. Y N

2. Add commas.

The flowers had pink purple and

blue petals.

4. Y N

___/ 4
Total

3. Write the correct verb.

_____

Alex _____ to go home.

(**want** or **wants**)

4. Unscramble the letters to make a word.

_____

l p i _____

DAY 160

NAME: _____

DIRECTIONS Read and answer each question.

SCORE

1. Circle the word that needs a capital letter.

Don't forget to come over on february 9!

2. Add commas.

I need to wear a hat a shirt and shoes.

3. Write the correct pronoun.

Maria and Ava wear _____ uniforms.

(**their** or **her**)

4. Unscramble the middle letters to make a word.

I s i t _____

1. Ⓨ Ⓝ
2. Ⓨ Ⓝ
3. Ⓨ Ⓝ
4. Ⓨ Ⓝ

___ / 4
Total

© Shell Education   #51166—180 Days of Language   171

NAME: _____

SCORE

1. Ⓨ Ⓝ

2. Ⓨ Ⓝ

3. Ⓨ Ⓝ

4. Ⓨ Ⓝ

___ / 4
Total

DIRECTIONS Read and answer each question.

1. What is the name of your teacher?

_____

- - - - - - - - - - - - - - - - - -

_____

2. Add commas.

I like to eat fruit vegetables and meat.

3. Circle the nouns.

The bottle for the baby is ready.

4. Circle the word that is spelled correctly.

upon   uponn   upawn

#51166—180 Days of Language

NAME: _____

DIRECTIONS Read and answer each question.

1. Circle the words that need capital letters.

Is grandma visiting on march 15?

2. Add punctuation.

I need shade from the

hot sun

3. Write the correct noun.

Your _____ are nice.

(**friend** or **friends**)

4. Unscramble the middle letters to make a word.

h v a e _____

NAME: _____

SCORE

DIRECTIONS Read and answer each question.

1. Y N

1. What is the name of your custodian?

_____

- - - - - - - - - - - - - - - - - - -

2. Y N

_____

3. Y N

2. Add punctuation.

Can I have more time to finish

4. Y N

___/ 4
Total

3. Write two adjectives about summer vacation.

_____

- - - - - - - - - - - - - - - - -

_____

- - - - - - - - - - - - - - - - -

_____

4. Unscramble the middle letters to make a word.

_____

m k a e - - - - - - - - - - - - - - - -

NAME: _____

DIRECTIONS Read and answer each question.

1. Circle the word that needs a capital letter.

1. Ⓨ Ⓝ

The project is due on october 22.

2. Ⓨ Ⓝ

2. Add punctuation.

3. Ⓨ Ⓝ

Do you know your eye color

4. Ⓨ Ⓝ

3. Use an apostrophe to write *the spark from the fire* in another way.

___ / 4
Total

_____

- - - - - - - - - - - - - - - - - -

_____

4. Unscramble the letters to make a word.

_____

- - - - - - - - - - - - - - - - - -

g e g

NAME: _____

DIRECTIONS   Read and answer each question.

1. Which word needs a capital letter? Write it correctly on the line.

today, we are having pizza for lunch.

_____

2. Add punctuation.

I ate tuna at lunch

3. Write the correct verb.

The clock _____ all day.
          (**ticks** or **tick**)

3. Unscramble the middle letters to make a word.

b s e t _____

NAME: _____

DIRECTIONS Read and answer each question.

1. Circle the word that needs a capital letter.

Who has a birthday on july 15?

2. Add a comma.

It is due on December 4 2015.

3. Write the correct pronoun.

Cindy loves _____ sister.
(their or **her)**

4. Unscramble the middle letters to make a word.

g v a e _____

NAME: _____

Read and answer each question.

SCORE

1. Ⓨ Ⓝ

2. Ⓨ Ⓝ

3. Ⓨ Ⓝ

4. Ⓨ Ⓝ

___ / 4
Total

1. What is the name of your principal?

_____

- - - - - - - - - - - - - - - - - -

_____

2. Write tomorrow's date.

_____

- - - - - - - - - - - - - - - - - -

_____

3. Use an apostrophe to write *the toy belonging to Evan* in another way.

_____

- - - - - - - - - - - - - - - - - -

_____

4. Which word is **not** spelled correctly?

hope   hoop   hopp

NAME: _____

DIRECTIONS Read and answer each question.

1. Circle the word that needs a capital letter.

Who has a special day on august 3?

2. Write yesterday's date.

_____

- - - - - - - - - - - - - - - -

_____

3. Write the present tense verb.

Jane _____ a prize.

(**wants** or **wanted**)

4. Which word is **not** spelled correctly?

tack   tak   take

NAME: _____

DIRECTIONS Read and answer each question.

1. Which word needs a capital letter? Write it correctly on the line.

when is our P.E. class starting?

_____

_____

2. Add punctuation.

Math is my favorite subject

3. Write two adjectives about football.

_____

_____

4. Which word is **not** spelled correctly?

path   patt   pat

NAME: _____

DIRECTIONS Read and answer each question.

1. Circle the word that needs a capital letter.

who is going to play?

2. Add punctuation.

What is second grade like

3. Write the present tense verb.

Brad _____ a skateboard.
(**owned** or **owns**)

4. Which word is **not** spelled correctly?

one   onc   once

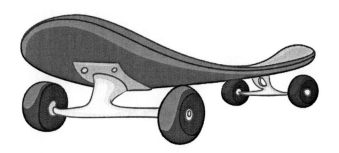

NAME: _____

DIRECTIONS Read and answer each question.

1. Circle the word that needs a capital letter.

Our birthdays are both on november 15!

2. Add commas.

February 14 2016 will be a great day.

3. Write the correct noun.

The _____ walks away.
(**man** or **men**)

4. Which word is **not** spelled correctly?

off   of   oof

NAME: _____

DIRECTIONS Read and answer each question.

1. Circle the words that need capital letters.

ben likes to talk to jan about books.

2. Add punctuation.

The fly buzzed and buzzed

3. Write the correct pronoun

Marcus does not want

_____

_ _ _ _ _ _ lunch.

(**he** or **his**)

4. Which word is **not** spelled correctly?

been   bin   bene

NAME: _____

DIRECTIONS   Read and answer each question.

1. Y N

1. Circle the words that need capital letters.

May I invite ron and henry?

2. Y N

2. Add punctuation.

The pet ran away

3. Y N

3. Write the correct verb.

4. Y N

Our family _____ dinner.

_____/ 4
Total

(**eats** or **ates**)

4. Which word is **not** spelled correctly?

ball   bill   bal

NAME: _____

DIRECTIONS Read and answer each question.

1. Circle the word that needs a capital letter.

My friend ella is smart.

2. Add punctuation.

I have never heard something

so loud

3. Write the present tense verb.

I am _____ the show.

(**watching** or **watched**)

4. Which word is **not** spelled correctly?

ask   ane   and

NAME: _____

DIRECTIONS Read and answer each question.

1. ⓎⓃ

2. ⓎⓃ

3. ⓎⓃ

4. ⓎⓃ

___ / 4
Total

1. Circle the words that need capital letters.

ben can play soccer with aiden.

2. Add punctuation.

Where did Ana go

3. Write the present tense verb.

The cow _____ in the field.
(**moved** or **moves**)

4. Which word is **not** spelled correctly?

mu   may   make

#51166—180 Days of Language   © Shell Education

NAME: _____

DIRECTIONS Read and answer each question.

1. Circle the words that need capital letters.

jenna plays video games

with sadie.

2. Add punctuation.

Can we go yet

3. Use an apostrophe to write *the house belonging to Sam* in another way.

_____

— — — — — — — — — — — — — —

_____

4. Which word is **not** spelled correctly?

life   lif   live

NAME: _____

SCORE

DIRECTIONS Read and answer each question.

1. Circle the words that need capital letters.

1. Ⓨ Ⓝ

han watches a show with his

2. Ⓨ Ⓝ

sister ling.

3. Ⓨ Ⓝ

2. Add punctuation.

4. Ⓨ Ⓝ

Who would do that

___/4
Total

3. Circle the verb.

I went to soccer practice.

4. Which word is **not** spelled correctly?

culd   cold   could

NAME: _____

DIRECTIONS Read and answer each question.

1. Circle the words that need capital letters.

mario and ramon are

best friends.

2. Add punctuation.

I am very scared

3. Write the correct noun.

The _____ is in trouble.
(**students** or **student**)

4. Which word is **not** spelled correctly?

him   hime   her

NAME: _____

1. Ⓨ Ⓝ

2. Ⓨ Ⓝ

3. Ⓨ Ⓝ

4. Ⓨ Ⓝ

___ / 4
Total

DIRECTIONS Read and answer each question.

1. Which are always capitalized?

names of months

adjectives

nouns

2. Add punctuation.

That movie made me scream

3. Write two adjectives about your favorite dessert.

_____

_____

4. Which word is **not** spelled correctly?

tak   tack   take

#51166—180 Days of Language

NAME: _____

DIRECTIONS Read and answer each question.

1. Which are always capitalized?

names of people

verbs

pronouns

2. Add punctuation.

We worked hard to finish

this book

3. Circle the nouns.

Harry and Sam play tennis.

4. Which word is **not** spelled correctly?

from   form   fom

ANSWER KEY

Note: Depending on how students read the sentences that ask for ending punctuation, you may have some students who put periods and some that put exclamation points. Teachers should grade student responses at their discretion.

Day 1
1. My friend **Sam** is funny.
2. Where are we going**?**
3. **I** want a new bike.
4. pick

Day 2
1. School will start on **August** 25.
2. I like to play soccer at recess.
3. The **girls** feel sad today.
4. use

Day 3
1. Answers will vary.
2. The music is loud**.**
3. Each day, I **walk** to school.
4. grin

Day 4
1. Mrs. **Walker** is my teacher.
2. Where is my book**?**
3. I like to sit in **red** chairs.
4. feeding

Day 5
1. My friend **Lily** was not at school.
2. I ate a lot at lunch**.**
3. Yesterday, I **ate** pizza.
4. you

Day 6
1. Today I will see **Dr. Martin**.
2. The cat is on the bed**.**
3. Dad told **me** to go to sleep.
4. step

Day 7
1. The ball game is on **May** 25.
2. When is recess**?**
3. **He** reads the book.
4. best

Day 8
1. I sit next to **Tim**.
2. I am very excited today**!**
3. **Zoe's** dog was missing.
4. hop

Day 9
1. The party is on **July** 6.
2. I love bananas**,** apples, and melons.
3. The **big** park was a lot of fun.
4. jet

Day 10
1. My sister **Greta** is nice.
2. I got books, pencils, and markers at the store.
3. Yesterday, I **spelled** all of the words.
4. fix

Day 11
1. Answers will vary.
2. School starts on August 24, 2016.
3. Put the **food** on the **table**.
4. deep

Day 12
1. **Dr. Kim** checks my teeth.
2. Answers will vary.
3. **Silly** songs make me laugh.
4. bone

Day 13
1. Is my party in **March** or **April**?
2. Our trip is on June 5, 2016.
3. Will you wash **Dad's** car?
4. time

Day 14
1. Answers will vary.
2. The bus stopped**.**
3. **He** runs to the door.
4. We need **roap** to tie the box.

Day 15
1. Answers will vary.
2. Where is Liam**?**
3. The desk is **between** Katy and me.
4. Can I go **wyth** Jessie?

Day 16
1. Answers will vary.
2. The puppy was born on October 4, 2016.
3. The **horse's** tail is long.
4. feet

Day 17
1. **I** am good at math.
2. The car has doors, wheels, and an engine.
3. Pillows are **fluffy**.
4. sock

Day 18
1. I play with **John** at recess.
2. We use paint, paper**,** and glue at art time.
3. **I** saw **Mr. Cortez** in the **classroom**.
4. doing

Day 19
1. Our librarian is **Mr. Perez**.
2. Answers will vary.
3. Yesterday, I **ate** a lot of fruit.
4. skip

Day 20
1. **We** are going on a trip.
2. Come home right now**!**
3. Yesterday, Anna **laughed** at her friend.
4. slam

Day 21
1. Is **June** or **July** your favorite month?
2. When is school over**?**
3. The **cat** ran away.
4. see

Day 22
1. She played with **Rose** and **Ted**.
2. The cake was made with eggs, milk, and butter.
3. The frog **hops**.
4. came

ANSWER KEY (cont.)

Day 23
1. My birthday month is **February**.
2. The dog ate his food**.**
3. Tomorrow, I will **keep** my promise.
4. hop

Day 24
1. I see that **Tim** and **Rex** play together.
2. We moved on March 4**,** 2014.
3. The **new** book was very good.
4. gave

Day 25
1. Today is the first day of **October**.
2. The circus was a lot of fun**!**
3. Chloe likes to play with **me**.
4. rode

Day 26
1. My friends are **Evan** and **Ned**.
2. Who is the line leader**?**
3. School was over**, but** the bus was not there.
4. doing

Day 27
1. How many days are left in **March**?
2. The music was very quiet**.**
3. **Hot** chocolate tastes good.
4. bugs

Day 28
1. I want to read with **Chris** or **Eva**.
2. My sister was born on August 7**,** 2014.
3. The sky **will be** very cloudy.
4. gets

Day 29
1. **Will** it be hot in **May**?
2. Camp starts on July 12**,** 2016.
3. Snow was falling**, and** the street was quiet.
4. this

Day 30
1. You must work with **Gus** and **Frank**.
2. I saw bugs**,** grass**,** and rocks at the park.
3. Dad and I rode **our** bikes.
4. telling

Day 31
1. My neighbor is **Bob Gomez**.
2. The flower grew in the pot**.**
3. I see **green** grass outside.
4. ride

Day 32
1. It is very cold in **January**.
2. The carnival was on April 15**,** 2013.
3. I have soccer practice**, but** I am hungry.
4. reading

Day 33
1. The bus driver today is **Alice Walters**.
2. I want ice cream**,** a cherry**,** and whipped cream.
3. Yesterday, I **played** at home.
4. frog

Day 34
1. **Mrs.** Holly **Evans** works in the cafeteria.
2. When is my soccer game**?**
3. **Large** whales swim around.
4. walked

Day 35
1. I am shy around **Dr. Perry**, my dentist.
2. What day of the week is June 4**,** 2014?
3. The **girl** dances to the song.
4. keeping

Day 36
1. **June** starts today.
2. That music sure is loud**.**
3. I hear **loud** cars.
4. spin

Day 37
1. **Chloe** and **Troy** work well together.
2. The jacket had pockets**,** buttons**,** and zippers.
3. Yesterday, I **added** numbers at math time.
4. of

Day 38
1. December
2. The coat kept her warm**.**
3. The spider **moves** slowly
4. seeing

Day 39
1. The month of **January** is first.
2. Next Sunday is September 12**,** 2015.
3. The **pretty** butterfly flew.
4. nose

Day 40
1. I will invite **Parker** and **Timmy**.
2. Where is Mom**?**
3. The **car** stops at the corner.
4. saying

Day 41
1. My friends are **Iris** and **Nina**.
2. How do you do that**?**
3. The **bee** zoomed by.
4. **This** is my lunch.

Day 42
1. When can I play with **Uncle Frank**?
2. The rug was blue**,** red**,** and green.
3. The **snakes** look for food.
4. bus

Day 43
1. May
2. Who needs to rest**?**
3. Yesterday, Mom **watched** the baby.
4. **That** book makes me laugh.

ANSWER KEY *(cont.)*

Day 44
1. My friend **Justin** is nice.
2. How many days until January 3, 2016?
3. Each day, I **walk** to the library.
4. I ride a **bike**.

Day 45
1. My **Aunt Ruth** is funny.
2. The story needs a beginning, a middle**,** and an end.
3. The **small** flower smells nice.
4. the

Day 46
1. March
2. Where do I go**?**
3. Anna wanted **her** roller skates.
4. said

Day 47
1. Uncle **Joe** and **Aunt Pam** are here.
2. That is very loud**!**
3. Trophies are **shiny**.
4. an

Day 48
1. Can we go away on **June** 15?
2. The pie was made with milk, sugar**,** and flour.
3. Yesterday, Ian **skipped** his homework.
4. come

Day 49
1. Our table group includes **Max** and **Brad**.
2. I am very mad**!**
3. The **large** fire was hot.
4. I see a **bug** go by.

Day 50
1. May
2. Do you want chocolate, vanilla, or strawberry ice cream?
3. The rain **means** no recess.
4. Can we **run** home?

Day 51
1. **I** like pizza.
2. Do you like bugs**?**
3. **Pretty** flowers grow in parks.
4. Say **yes** or no.

Day 52
1. Are you coming over, **Anna**?
2. My birthday is June 4, 2016.
3. Today, I **saw** a parrot.
4. The **jet** was fast.

Day 53
1. I
2. Riley, Oscar**,** and Jose are in line.
3. Tomorrow, I **will talk** to her.
4. saying

Day 54
1. I saw **Dr. Evan** and **Dr. Parker** at the store.
2. Hank, Anna**,** and Cole are on the bus.
3. The ant **steps** over the rock.
4. The **top** of the pot was off.

Day 55
1. The play is on **March** 5 and **March** 6.
2. Mark the calendar for January 5, 2018.
3. Classrooms are **fun**.
4. since

Day 56
1. **The** plane leaves on **May** 25.
2. The rose is red**.**
3. Nina loves **stuffed** bears.
4. camping

Day 57
1. Will I see **Mr. Roberts** today?
2. I need a new hat**.**
3. Amanda **finds** a dollar bill.
4. I see the **rip** in the coat.

Day 58
1. I love my **Grandpa Joe** and my **Grandma Alana**.
2. When is school out**?**
3. Can you help out while **we** go away?
4. Can the dog **flip** over?

Day 59
1. **Can** we have a party on **May** 15?
2. How are you doing**?**
3. The **early** sunrise was pretty.
4. I like the **end** of the story.

Day 60
1. **Paul, Ron,** and **Taylor** are coming over.
2. I am very happy**!**
3. The girl **walks** home.
4. job

Day 61
1. Answers will vary.
2. I cannot wait for summer**!**
3. The baby will sleep**, but** first he needs milk.
4. My **nose** keeps running.

Day 62
1. **Let's** go for a walk.
2. Where is my hat**?**
3. The **girl** walked to her **house**.
4. going

Day 63
1. Is **Paul** out sick today?
2. That really hurt**!**
3. The **dogs** are happy.
4. Please **rake** the yard.

Day 64
1. Our coach, **Mario**, was happy today.
2. The lizard is green**.**
3. The **child** sits at the desk.
4. know

Day 65
1. Did **Nurse Chris** come in yet?
2. The water is cold**.**
3. I like to wake up early **because** I like mornings.
4. can

Day 66
1. Answers will vary.
2. We had food, towels**,** and toys at the beach.
3. The class **plays** a game.
4. open

ANSWER KEY (cont.)

Day 67
1. My piano teacher is **Mrs. Oliver**.
2. February 14, 2016
3. Friends are **nice**.
4. sock

Day 68
1. Answers will vary.
2. Green, red, and blue are my favorite colors.
3. **I** went inside with Mary.
4. helping

Day 69
1. **November** 29, 2016
2. June 18, 2015, will be a great day.
3. The team **lost** the game.
4. again

Day 70
1. Answers will vary.
2. Let's make a fort out of pillows, blankets, and towels.
3. I **went** under the desk.
4. thank

Day 71
1. Today is **January** 4, 2015.
2. December 25, 2015
3. The bird **moved** its wings.
4. give

Day 72
1. Answers will vary.
2. Mom put cheese, an apple, and chips in my lunch.
3. I will **stay** in the car.
4. when

Day 73
1. Tuesday
2. August 1, 2000
3. The **bird** flew out of the **window**.
4. walk

Day 74
1. Answers will vary.
2. We all need water, food, and air to live.
3. The **nice** party was fun.
4. The sign says to **stop**.

Day 75
1. Brett
2. Is our vacation on May 13, 2016?
3. **I** open the door to go inside.
4. A **grin** means you are happy.

Day 76
1. Answers will vary.
2. Today is Monday.
3. Joe likes **his** pet, Rex.
4. zoo

Day 77
1. Do we go on **May** 4 or **June** 4?
2. It will be January 6, 2016 soon.
3. The dog **runs** at the park.
4. The dog must **sit**.

Day 78
1. Answers will vary.
2. Who needs a pen?
3. The fish **moved**.
4. room

Day 79
1. Is **June** or **July** coming up next?
2. Answers will vary.
3. I see **him** at home.
4. I am **his** friend.

Day 80
1. Answers will vary.
2. You are very funny!
3. The fastest **runner** wins.
4. soon

Day 81
1. Answers will vary.
2. Our flag is red, white, and blue.
3. The **small** tree is growing.
4. The girls **ran** to play.

Day 82
1. Answers will vary.
2. Let's play with a ball, a bat, and a mitt.
3. Our dog **runs** on the beach.
4. box

Day 83
1. Answers will vary.
2. The game will be on June 4, 2016.
3. Paula misses **her** friend.
4. Who **had** the book first?

Day 84
1. Our next school holiday is in **October**.
2. January 15, 2016 will be a special day.
3. The **car** is blue.
4. The **pot** may be very hot.

Day 85
1. Answers will vary.
2. I asked my mom for cheese, bananas, and crackers for lunch.
3. The waves **crash** on the sand.
4. such

Day 86
1. Answers will vary.
2. The dog loves to walk.
3. The dog **smelled** the grass.
4. bone

Day 87
1. Answers will vary.
2. Ted has red, purple, and blue crayons.
3. The ball lands in **a** bush.
4. keep

Day 88
1. Answers will vary.
2. Who wants to be my partner?
3. My mom told **me** to be safe.
4. Let's play with **them**!

Day 89
1. Answers will vary.
2. The bus driver told us to keep arms, legs, and heads inside.
3. The **ball** flew over the **net**.
4. push

Day 90
1. Answers will vary.
2. That yelling is way too loud!
3. The **tigers** growl.
4. **Where** are you going?

ANSWER KEY (cont.)

Day 91
1. Answers will vary.
2. Leap Day is on February 29, 2016.
3. There are **yummy** treats at **surprise** parties.
4. Please put the cup **here**.

Day 92
1. Answers will vary.
2. How did you get to school**?**
3. Sam is **sweet**.
4. Answers will vary.

Day 93
1. Answers will vary.
2. What will we do on January 4, 2016?
3. The **sled** was very fast.
4. The cat is **by** the fence.

Day 94
1. Answers will vary.
2. This math game is fun**.**
3. I **rode** past the park.
4. Answers will vary.

Day 95
1. Answers will vary.
2. The cafeteria has milk**,** water, and juice.
3. The bunny **hops** away.
4. Answers will vary.

Day 96
1. Answers will vary.
2. Where is my lunch**?**
3. Yesterday, **I** ate a salad.
4. Answers will vary.

Day 97
1. **Today**, **I** want to go to the movies.
2. Where will you be on May 5, 2016?
3. My **old** dog does not like to run.
4. Answers will vary.

Day 98
1. I will ask **Mrs.** Jones a question.
2. I am very excited for the sleepover**!**
3. How did you **feel**?
4. Answers will vary.

Day 99
1. I am going on a trip in **July**.
2. I ate rice**,** beans**,** and salsa for dinner.
3. The band played **loud** music.
4. every

Day 100
1. Answers will vary.
2. My party is on March 3**,** 2015.
3. **I** did not see the boy until **he** ran out.
4. round

Day 101
1. February 21
2. Where is our teacher**?**
3. Pam loves **small**, **blue** birds.
4. Sam wants **some** food.

Day 102
1. March 14
2. October 14, 2015
3. Kai **steps** outside.
4. The **life** of a horse lasts many years.

Day 103
1. April 21
2. The pig slept in the sun**.**
3. Chloe eats ice cream**, or** she eats cake.
4. When will we **know**?

Day 104
1. July 5
2. May 9**,** 2016
3. Evan had practice**, but** he didn't want to go.
4. walk

Day 105
1. October 1
2. Who can water the garden**?**
3. The spider **moves** on the web.
4. Answers will vary.

Day 106
1. I want to play with **Ernie**.
2. When will school start**?**
3. **Ava's** sister went to bed.
4. Can you spot the **bat**?

Day 107
1. **Mr. Evans** wants to see me.
2. The bunny hopped away**.**
3. Pam left, but **she** forgot her lunch.
4. Answers will vary.

Day 108
1. The teacher told **Nico** to get to work.
2. Mark the calendar for October 25, 2016.
3. **The farmer** feeds the cows.
4. please

Day 109
1. My coach, **Brad**, was not happy today.
2. The band played drums**,** piano, and guitar.
3. **Ruby's** coat was nice.
4. Answers will vary.

Day 110
1. When will **Ella** be able to play?
2. The plant was tall, green**,** and healthy.
3. The animals **moved** the train.
4. have

Day 111
1. My mom has a birthday on **May** 2.
2. Chloe is tall, smart**,** and kind.
3. the tree's nest
4. Please do not get **hurt**.

Day 112
1. My dad comes home on **July** 24.
2. Jake's car was red**,** shiny, and fast.
3. The **chair** is beside the **desk**.
4. Answers will vary.

ANSWER KEY *(cont.)*

Day 113
1. Can **Cole** stack the toys for me?
2. The cookies had sugar**,** salt**,** and flour.
3. Answers will vary.
4. Marco can **toss** the ball to Sid.

Day 114
1. When will **Olivia** be home?
2. Faith's hat
3. Answers will vary.
4. Answers will vary.

Day 115
1. Why did **Liam** have to go home?
2. the teacher's book
3. Sally can go to the pool**,** **or** she can go to the park.
4. Make sure to wash the **pan**.

Day 116
1. Why is **Milo** mad at me?
2. Karen saw a bug in her room**.**
3. Iris had to do her homework**,** **but** she ate first.
4. Answers will vary.

Day 117
1. I know that **Dr. Fisher** is very kind.
2. I turn 10 on January 29, 2019.
3. Sara's sister
4. Answers will vary.

Day 118
1. I have to see **Dr. Baxter** tomorrow.
2. Who is in the car**?**
3. Lila's teacher was gone on Friday.
4. Answers will vary.

Day 119
1. I think that **Mrs. Harris** is a great teacher.
2. Watch out for the rock**!**
3. Dan likes to ride **his** bike.
4. path

Day 120
1. Our team likes **Coach Sandy**.
2. I think you should go home**.**
3. Answers will vary.
4. Answers will vary.

Day 121
1. I need help with my homework from **Jamie**.
2. Do you think I can do that**?**
3. Carter did not **feel** well.
4. fur

Day 122
1. Our principal is **Mrs. Sanchez**.
2. Do not let go of the rope**!**
3. Juan's game
4. fost

Day 123
1. The first grade teachers are **Mrs. Johns** and **Mr. Paulson**.
2. I am hungry**.**
3. The artist **made** a painting.
4. rhuck

Day 124
1. **Abby** and **Max** are good friends.
2. Why are you mad**?**
3. Kara and **I** walked to school.
4. tep

Day 125
1. I hope that **Jake** can fix my bike.
2. I cannot wait for recess**!**
3. The sisters **argue** over the game.
4. our

Day 126
1. I want **Nate** to come over.
2. How will I get that done**?**
3. I **pour** my milk into the glass.
4. The pool is too **deep**.

Day 127
1. October 6
2. That is very scary**!**
3. **We** are such good friends.
4. fap

Day 128
1. My mom is named **Lily**.
2. The sunset at the beach was pretty**.**
3. Nina's art was hung on the wall.
4. It is my job to **feed** our cat.

Day 129
1. Save the treat for **April** 2.
2. The plant needs water and sun**.**
3. Answers will vary.
4. sep

Day 130
1. My sister **Ann** wants a snack.
2. Where is my glass**?**
3. The **dog** and **cat** like to play.
4. She **came** to bed after the show.

Day 131
1. Answers will vary.
2. Who can come over today**?**
3. The baby **cries** when he is tired.
4. very

Day 132
1. Answers will vary.
2. I am feeling very happy**!**
3. Parker thought **he** heard a noise.
4. Dad **rode** his bike to work.

Day 133
1. Answers will vary.
2. The cake had red**,** pink**,** and blue frosting.
3. Claire **swims** in the pool.
4. because

Day 134
1. Answers will vary.
2. My mom made rice**,** chicken**,** and carrots.
3. My **friend's** mom is nice.
4. Juan can **hop** on one foot.

Day 135
1. Answers will vary.
2. We need glue**,** paper**,** and scissors for the project.
3. Jack's dad **took** us to school.
4. Answers will vary.

ANSWER KEY *(cont.)*

Day 136
1. Answers will vary.
2. The book has action, suspense, and mystery.
3. The kids **liked** to ride bikes.
4. Dad cooks in a **pan**.

Day 137
1. Don't forget to come on **July** 24.
2. Please bring water, a ball, and a snack to practice.
3. Our choir **sings** in the show.
4. going

Day 138
1. Tomorrow will be **August** 3.
2. The big game will be on June 5, 2015.
3. The teachers **decide** to give a test.
4. Answers will vary.

Day 139
1. March 10
2. We have to move on May 15, 2016.
3. The **scientists** see the **dolphins**.
4. once

Day 140
1. December 1
2. Our school closes on June 15, 2014.
3. Answers will vary.
4. Answers will vary.

Day 141
1. Answers will vary.
2. Can you fix the window?
3. The rain **stops**.
4. eating

Day 142
1. I had lunch with **Grandpa Bill** and **Grandma Maria**.
2. Do you like to eat vegetables?
3. Please get your **work** done soon.
4. heer

Day 143
1. Answers will vary.
2. The calendar stops on December 31, 2015.
3. The baby **finds** his mother.
4. tael

Day 144
1. months
2. There are ants, spiders, and other bugs outside.
3. Sylvia **walked** her dog.
4. ower

Day 145
1. Answers will vary.
2. We need fans, water, and ice to stay cool.
3. I can have pizza **and** I can have milk; I can have pizza **and** milk.
4. meit

Day 146
1. Both **Uncle Bob** and **Uncle Carlos** came to my party.
2. The hive was buzzing.
3. Chris **baked** a cake.
4. flat

Day 147
1. Answers will vary.
2. Why does this always happen?
3. Kara's lunch box
4. step

Day 148
1. Is our field trip on **May** 4 or **June** 4?
2. The beach was very dirty.
3. **Cheesy** pizza is **delicious**.
4. drop

Day 149
1. Answers will vary.
2. How can we get home?
3. The lions **run** very fast.
4. slab

Day 150
1. The play will be on **May** 4.
2. This is the best day ever!
3. Kevin's aunt took care of me.
4. clap

Day 151
1. Answers will vary.
2. Who is your teacher?
3. Answers will vary.
4. plan

Day 152
1. Answers will vary.
2. The car zoomed by!
3. Zia asked to have **her** friends over.
4. trip

Day 153
1. Answers will vary.
2. Where is your house?
3. The **cops** work very hard.
4. slug

Day 154
1. Answers will vary.
2. The story had characters named Fred, Ted, and Ned.
3. the scientist's time machine
4. grin

Day 155
1. Answers will vary.
2. I want to go home, go to the pool, and go to the park.
3. The **boat** came to **shore**.
4. clip

Day 156
1. I have to see **Dr. Walker** and **Dr. Martinez** about my broken arm.
2. Answers will vary.
3. Pablo loves to play with **his** brother.
4. clap

Day 157
1. Answers will vary.
2. Answers will vary.
3. A car **drives** by the store.
4. cone or once

Day 158
1. Answers will vary.
2. I will go to the park.
3. The band **travels**.
4. play

ANSWER KEY *(cont.)*

Day 159
1. Answers will vary.
2. The flowers had pink, purple, and blue petals.
3. Alex **wants** to go home.
4. lip

Day 160
1. Don't forget to come over on **February** 9!
2. I need to wear a hat, a shirt, and shoes.
3. Maria and Ava wear **their** uniforms.
4. list

Day 161
1. Answers will vary.
2. I like to eat fruit, vegetables, and meat.
3. The **bottle** for the **baby** is ready.
4. upon

Day 162
1. Is **Grandma** visiting on **March** 15?
2. I need shade from the hot sun.
3. Your **friends** are nice.
4. have

Day 163
1. Answers will vary.
2. Can I have more time to finish?
3. Answers will vary.
4. make

Day 164
1. The project is due on **October** 22.
2. Do you know your eye color?
3. the fire's spark
4. egg

Day 165
1. Today
2. I ate tuna at lunch.
3. The clock **ticks** all day.
4. best

Day 166
1. Who has a birthday on **July** 15?
2. It is due on December 4, 2015.
3. Cindy loves **her** sister.
4. gave

Day 167
1. Answers will vary.
2. Answers will vary.
3. Evan's toy
4. hopp

Day 168
1. Who has a special day on **August** 3?
2. Answers will vary.
3. Jane **wants** a prize.
4. tak

Day 169
1. When
2. Math is my favorite subject.
3. Answers will vary.
4. patt

Day 170
1. **Who** is going to the play?
2. What is second grade like?
3. Brad **owns** a skateboard.
4. onc

Day 171
1. Our birthdays are both on **November** 15!
2. February 14, 2016, will be a great day.
3. The **man** walks away.
4. oof

Day 172
1. **Ben** likes to talk to **Jan** about books.
2. The fly buzzed and buzzed.
3. Marcus does not want **his** lunch.
4. bene

Day 173
1. May I invite **Ron** and **Henry**?
2. The pet ran away.
3. Our family **eats** dinner.
4. bal

Day 174
1. My friend **Ella** is smart.
2. I have never heard something so loud!
3. I am **watching** the show.
4. ane

Day 175
1. **Ben** can play soccer with **Aiden**.
2. Where did Ana go?
3. The cow **moves** in the field.
4. mu

Day 176
1. **Jenna** plays video games with **Sadie**.
2. Can we go yet?
3. Sam's house
4. lif

Day 177
1. **Han** watches a show with his sister **Ling**.
2. Who would do that?
3. I **went** to soccer practice.
4. culd

Day 178
1. **Mario** and **Ramon** are best friends.
2. I am very scared!
3. The **student** is in trouble.
4. hime

Day 179
1. names of months
2. That movie made me scream!
3. Answers will vary.
4. tak

Day 180
1. names of people
2. We worked hard to finish this book.
3. **Harry** and **Sam** play **tennis**.
4. fom

My Language Book

by

_____

- -

_____

Capitalization

Always capitalize the **first word in a sentence**.

Example: The cat ran.

Always capitalize the word *I*.

Example: Do I need to go?

Always capitalize **names of people**.

Example: My friend's name is Kyle.

Always capitalize the **days of the week.**

Example: Today is Monday.

Always capitalize **months of the year**.

Example: It rains in June.

Always capitalize **names of holidays**.

Example: I cannot wait for Earth Day!

Punctuation

Symbol	Definition
. **period**	A **period** means the sentence is finished.
? **question mark**	A **question mark** means the sentence is a question.
! **exclamation point**	An **exclamation point** means there is strong feeling in the sentence.
, **comma**	A **comma** separates words or parts in a sentence.
" " **quotation marks**	**Quotation marks** mean someone is speaking.

Parts of Speech

A **noun** is the name of a person, an animal, a place, or a thing. It is also the subject in a sentence.

Example: The <u>dog</u> ran.

A **plural noun** means there is more than one noun.

Example: The <u>dogs</u> ran.

A **pronoun** takes the place of a noun.

Example: <u>He</u> ran.

A **verb** is the word in a sentence that names an action.

Example: I <u>play</u> at the park.

An **adjective** describes a noun.

Example: <u>The</u> flower is <u>red</u>.

An **adverb** describes a verb or an adjective.

Example 1: He walks <u>slowly</u>.

Example 2: The flower is <u>very</u> red.

Spelling

List 1	List 2	List 3	List 4
the	or	will	number
of	one	up	no
and	had	other	way
a	by	about	could
to	words	out	people
in	but	many	my
is	not	then	than
you	what	them	first
that	all	these	water
it	were	so	been
he	we	some	called
was	when	her	who
for	your	would	oil
on	can	make	sit
are	said	like	now
as	there	him	find
with	use	into	long
his	an	time	down
they	each	has	day
I	which	look	did
at	she	two	get
be	do	more	come
this	how	write	made
have	their	go	may
from	if	see	part

Dr. Fry's 1000 Instant Words © 2004 Teacher Created Materials

Spelling

List 5	List 6	List 7	List 8
over	say	set	try
new	great	put	kind
sound	where	end	hand
take	help	does	picture
only	through	another	again
little	much	well	change
work	before	large	off
know	line	must	play
place	right	big	spell
years	too	even	air
live	means	such	away
me	old	because	animal
back	any	turn	house
give	same	here	point
most	tell	why	page
very	boy	ask	letter
after	follow	went	mother
things	came	men	answer
our	want	read	found
just	show	need	study
name	also	land	still
good	around	different	learn
sentence	form	home	should
man	three	us	America
think	small	move	world

Dr. Fry's 1000 Instant Words © 2004 Teacher Created Materials

Spelling

List 9	List 10	List 11	List 12
high	saw	important	miss
every	left	until	idea
near	don't	children	enough
add	few	side	eat
food	while	feet	face
between	along	car	watch
own	might	mile	far
below	close	night	Indian
country	something	walk	real
plant	seem	white	almost
last	next	sea	let
school	hard	began	above
father	open	grow	girl
keep	example	took	sometimes
tree	begin	river	mountains
never	life	four	cut
start	always	carry	young
cry	those	state	talk
earth	both	once	soon
eyes	paper	book	list
light	together	hear	song
thought	got	stop	being
head	group	without	leave
under	often	second	family
story	run	late	it's

Dr. Fry's 1000 Instant Words © 2004 Teacher Created Materials

REFERENCES CITED

Haussamen, Brock. 2014. "Some Questions and Answers About Grammar." Retrieved from http://www.ateg.org/grammar/qna.php.

Hillocks, George, Jr., and Michael W. Smith. 1991. "Grammar and Usage." In *Handbook of Research on Teaching the English Language Arts*. James Flood, Julie M. Jensen, Diane Lapp, and James R. Squire. New York: Macmillan.

Hodges, Richard E. 1991. "The Conventions of Writing." In *Handbook of Research on Teaching the English Language Arts*. James Flood, Julie M. Jensen, Diane Lapp, and James R. Squire. New York: Macmillan.

———. 2003. "Grammar and Literacy Learning." In *Handbook of Research on Teaching the English Language Arts*, 2nd ed. James Flood, Julie M. Jensen, Diane Lapp, and James R. Squire. New York: Macmillan.

Lederer, Richard. 1987. *Anguished English: An Anthology of Accidental Assaults upon Our Language.* New York: Dell.

Marzano, Robert J. 2010. When Practice Makes Perfect. . .Sense. *Educational Leadership* 68(3): 81–83.

Truss, Lynne. 2003. *Eats, Shoots and Leaves: The Zero Tolerance Approach to Punctuation.* New York: Gotham Books.

CONTENTS OF THE DIGITAL RESOURCE CD

Teacher Resources

Resource	Filename
Diagnostic Assessment Directions	directions.pdf
Practice Page Item Analysis	pageitem.pdf pageitem.doc pageitem.xls
Student Item Analysis	studentitem.pdf studentitem.doc studentitem.xls
Standards Chart	standards.pdf

Student Resources

All of the 180 practice pages are contained in a single PDF. In order to print specific days, open the PDF and select the pages to print.

Resource	Filename
Practice Pages Day 1–Day 180	practicepages.pdf
My Language Book	languagebook.pdf